TURNER **CLASSIC** MOVIES.

A STAR IS BORN

Judy Garland and the Film that Got Away

LORNA LUFT

and JEFFREY VANCE

PHOTOGRAPHIC EDITOR: MATT TUNIA

RUNNING PRESS
PHILADELPHIA

Pages 2-3: Judy Garland during a music recording session for *A Star Is Born* (1954). Photo by Sanford Roth

Page 5: Portrait by John Engstead.

Page 6: Judy Garland portrait by John Engstead used to promote *A Star Is Born* (1954).

Running Press
Hachette Book Group
1290 Avenue of the Americas, New York, NY 10104
www.runningpress.com
@Running_Press

Printed in China

First Edition: September 2018

Published by Running Press, an imprint of Perseus Books, LLC, a subsidiary of Hachette Book Group, Inc. The Running Press name and logo is a trademark of the Hachette Book Group.

The Hachette Speakers Bureau provides a wide range of authors for speaking events. To find out more, go to www.hachettespeakersbureau.com or call (866) 376-6591.

The publisher is not responsible for websites (or their content) that are not owned by the publisher.

The "Oscar" statuette © Academy of Motion Picture Arts and Sciences® "OSCAR®," "OSCARS®," "ACADEMY AWARD®," "ACADEMY AWARDS®," and the "Oscar" design mark are trademarks and service marks of the Academy of Motion Picture Arts and Sciences

Print book cover and interior design by Susan Van Horn.

Library of Congress Control Number: 2018938089

ISBNs: 978-0-7624-6481-4 (hardcover), 978-0-7624-6480-7 (ebook)

1010

10 9 8 7 6 5 4 3 2 1

To my husband Colin;
my children Jesse,
Jaimee, Vanessa,
and Patrick;
and my grandchildren
Jordan, Luke, and Logan.
Every time I look at you,
a star is born.

—LORNA LUFT

To Jon S. Bouker.

—JEFFREY VANCE

CONTENTS

PREFACE

I PURSUED THE IDEA OF THIS BOOK TO CELEBRATE MY FAMILY TREE—a tree of entertainers, that begins with my grandparents owning the only movie theater in Grand Rapids, Minnesota, and whose branches grew all the way to my sister and myself. These branches have spread throughout my mother's legion of fans, from ages eight, to eighty, and beyond. Millions have been mesmerized, awed, and entertained by her movies, recordings, television shows, and concerts. And by her earth-shaking talent, charisma, and artistry.

Our family tree is a vision of beauty, strength, love, commitment, and resilience. It has also been a lightning rod for tragedy and sadness. More than anything however, this tree has always been a beacon of hope for myself, my children, my grandchildren, and for everyone that can look up toward the sky and experience *A Star Is Born*.

My coauthor, Jeffrey Vance, and I have been working on this project on and off since 2010. As a film historian and author of several books on the history of film, he is the perfect person to explain the genesis of *A Star Is Born* and how this book came about, which you will find in the Introduction.

—LORNA LUFT, RANCHO MIRAGE, 2018

⟩⟩ ◆ ⟨⟨

OPPOSITE: A pensive portrait of Judy Garland taken during production of *A Star Is Born* (1954). Photo by Bob Willoughby.

INTRODUCTION

"A CAREER IS A CURIOUS THING," NORMAN MAINE TELLS ESTHER Blodgett, brilliantly portrayed by Judy Garland, early in George Cukor's *A Star Is Born* (1954). "Talent isn't always enough. You need a sense of timing—an eye for seeing the turning point—for recognizing the big chance when it comes and grabbing it." *A Star Is Born* depicts the perfect storm of a great chance and the luminous talent to realize it. But despite the confluence of genius and ambition that find themselves simultaneously portrayed and manifested within *A Star Is Born*, the film failed to achieve the Hollywood apotheosis desired by its star, Judy Garland and its producer, Michael Sidney Luft (known as Sid Luft). This book tells the compelling story of the making of *A Star Is Born*, the film that was to be Garland's crowning achievement but instead—and undeservedly—marked the end of her great career as a motion picture star.

The main focus of our book recounts the behind-the-scenes narrative of the making of Judy Garland's *A Star Is Born*, and explores the film's successes and failures. It has been a long gestating project for Lorna, who visited the film set as a baby, and jokes that *A Star Is Born* is the closest her parents ever came to making a "home movie." Lorna's informal conversations with the film's costar, James Mason, augment memories and tales of the production heard from her parents. Newfound information has been culled from the massive amount of documentation that survives in the Warner Bros. Archives held at the University of Southern California and the many relevant collections of papers (including those of director George Cukor) held by the Margaret Herrick Library of the Academy of Motion Picture Arts and Sciences. My collaboration with Lorna began in 2010, when she encouraged me to interview people associated with Judy Garland and *A Star Is Born*, including the various notables who attended the film's extraordinary star-studded Hollywood premiere. Over the next two years, I was able to speak with thirty people. Over a third of these interview subjects have since passed on. Those precious interviews, whether referenced or not, have informed the text in myriad ways.

The book's illustrations draw mainly from Lorna's own extensive collection, and many have never before been published. The majority of these photographs derive from a complete keybook set of all the behind-the-scenes stills taken by the film's unit photographer, Pat Clark. Important images from special shoots by celebrated photographers Robert "Bob" Willoughby, Sanford H. Roth, and John Engstead supplement Lorna's materials, along with classic scene stills, frame enlargements, and ephemera, to chronicle the *A Star Is Born* story both in words and images.

A Star Is Born is a film with a rich history and one of Hollywood's favorite stories since 1932, when the precursor film, George Cukor's *What Price Hollywood?*, was released to theaters. Director William A. Wellman did his own version in 1937, rechristening it *A Star Is Born*, and actress Barbra Streisand produced her own rendition in 1976. I have included essays on all of these productions, to provide context for Judy Garland's film.

Even when *What Price Hollywood?* was conceived in the early sound era, movies about the movies were nothing new. Hollywood always has been fond of self-regard, and, sometimes, self-flagellation, reflecting back its own image comically, tragically, and—with the advent of "talkies"—musically. In the *ancien régime* of Hollywood, Charles Chaplin conjured comedy shorts such as the one-reel *The Masquerader* (1914) and *A Film Johnnie* (1914), as well as the two-reelers *His New Job* (1915) and *Behind the Screen* (1916), depicting the behind-the-scenes workings of moviemaking. Notable silent feature-length films with a backdrop of Hollywood include Maurice Tourneur's *A Girl's Folly* (1917), the

Judy Garland with daughter Lorna Luft, 1953. Photo by John Engstead.

11

Hollywood always has been fond of self-regard, and, some-times, self-flagellation, reflecting back its own image comically, tragically, and—with the advent of "talkies"—musically.

Mabel Normand starring vehicle *The Extra Girl* (1923), Rupert Hughes's *Souls for Sale* (1923), James Cruze's *Hollywood* (1923), the Colleen Moore–starring production *Ella Cinders* (1926), and King Vidor's *Show People* (1928), starring Marion Davies.

What Price Hollywood? was the most significant self-examination of Hollywood culture of the early talking-film period. Other notable film-centric films of the 1930s include Raoul Walsh's *Going Hollywood* (1933) starring Marion Davies and Bing Crosby and *Hollywood Hotel* (1937), both musicals of the *42nd Street* (1933) variety. *Hollywood Cavalcade* (1939) is a nostalgic view of Hollywood's early days and employs many silent-film veterans. The next decade produced at least one outstanding Hollywood tale: Preston Sturges's *Sullivan's Travels* (1941), which concerns a movie director, disillusioned with Hollywood high-style comedy, who hobos through the countryside in search of true-to-life inspiration.

In the 1950s, Hollywood looked in the mirror more often. Billy Wilder's *Sunset Boulevard* (1950) delves into the deepening madness of fictitious silent movie queen Norma Desmond, played by real-life silent movie queen Gloria Swanson. Nicholas Ray's film noir *In a Lonely Place* (1950) involves a tormented screenwriter suspected of murder. Vincente Minnelli's *The Bad and the Beautiful* (1952) features four former studio colleagues who reflect on the flexible ethical standards of their industry. Hollywood history and pretense are satirized in the musical comedy brilliance of Stanley Donen and Gene Kelly's *Singin' in the Rain* (1952).

After the 1950s, the notable films reflecting moviemaking culture decrease in number but nevertheless include such greats as Federico Fellini's *8½* (1963), the filmmaker's avant-garde autobiographical exploration of a director experiencing a creative block, while François

Truffaut's *Day for Night* (1973) presents the professional and personal problems facing the cast and crew during production of a movie; *The Stunt Man* (1980) features a fugitive of the law who stumbles onto a movie set and becomes a stuntman for the film's autocratic director; and Robert Altman's *The Player* (1992) is a black comedy (containing many celebrity cameos) in which a film executive murders a screenwriter, courts his girlfriend, and gets away with the crime, while ending up the head of the studio. Tim Burton's *Ed Wood* (1994) is a celebration of movie-making as practiced by the low-budget filmmaker Ed Wood. Martin Scorsese's *Hugo* (2011) delves into the creative world of film pioneer Georges Méliès. Michel Hazanavicius's *The Artist* (2011) reconsiders the falling movie idol/rising star fable, but transfers it to Hollywood of the silent-film era and gives it a happy ending. *The Artist* is an *homage* to the original *A Star Is Born* story, made by a French director and with two French stars, filmed on location in Los Angeles. It is an outsider's valentine to the enduringly fertile, derided, yet beloved setting: Hollywood. *La La Land* (2016) muses on the power, but also the fragility, of dreams, sets those dreams to music, and ravishingly photographs them in real Los Angeles locations. All of these movies draw on Hollywood life as it was formed in the first half of the twentieth century: Some were cautionary tales; others chronicled the myths that quickly grew up around the motion picture industry and the culture it engendered.

Other artistic forms have also explored the American film industry. Predating *What Price Hollywood?*, *Merton of the Movies*, a 1922 novel by Harry Lean Wilson was adapted into a successful Broadway play by George S. Kaufman and Marc Connelly. (*Merton of the Movies* was adapted into a feature film in 1924 and again in 1947.) Another key theatrical work in this genre is Moss Hart and George S. Kaufman's 1930 Broadway hit *Once in a Lifetime*, a satirical comedy about Hollywood during the transition to sound. (Moss Hart also wrote the script for Garland's version of *A Star Is Born*.) No serious consideration of the literature concerning the American movie industry would be complete without mentioning such superb novels as F. Scott Fitzgerald's unfinished *roman à clef* of 1930s Hollywood *The Last Tycoon*; Nathanael West's 1939 *The Day of the Locust*; and Budd Schulberg's 1941 *What Makes Sammy Run?*

Hollywood culture during the studio system even enjoyed a serious ethnographic examination. Anthropologist Hortense Powdermaker's 1950 text *Hollywood: The Dream Factory*, remains a fascinating study of the American film industry as it existed in the late 1940s.

Holding a special place across the decades of classic films, important novels, and theatrical works that stand alongside it, *A Star Is Born* continues to resonate. What is it about the *Star Is Born* story that proves so compelling as to always find it being remade? One answer is that, at its basic level, it examines the father/daughter dynamic. This would have appealed to Judy Garland due to her unresolved relationship to her own father and also relates to her own marriage, as the older man nurturing the younger woman certainly reflects aspects of the Sid Luft–Judy Garland relationship. But while the tale told in *A Star Is Born* in any iteration no doubt boasts many superlative elements, it is Judy Garland that audiences remember. This is attributable

---

Garland's impressive relaunch of her brand included triumphant concert engagements at the London Palladium and New York City's Palace Theatre in 1951–1952.

---

not only to the film as a showcase for her immeasurable talents, but also to the sentimental mirroring of reality for Judy Garland herself within the narrative, especially as it relates to her comeback to films after a four-year absence.

A Star Is Born was Garland's turning point, but was also George Cukor's. The film was the director's first musical, his first film in color, and his first in the widescreen format. The ambitious project was met with much skepticism within the industry. Judy Garland's career— beset by severe personal and professional setbacks, which included dependency on prescription

OPPOSITE: Garland touches up her makeup during a break in filming the famous "Born in a Trunk" sequence of *A Star Is Born* (1954). Photo by Bob Willoughby.

medication, unreliability at the studio, suicide attempts, and depressive episodes that left her unable to function—appeared to be moribund by 1950, only to be reawakened that year by the magical kiss of her crafty Prince Charming, Sid Luft. As Garland contemplated some kind of show business return, she and her new partner in the "Judy Garland business," realized that there was not enough money in radio; she had no record contract; and television was in its infancy (not to mention that she had no interest in the medium). Garland's impressive relaunch of her brand included triumphant concert engagements at the London Palladium and New York City's Palace Theatre in 1951–1952. After the successes of her live performances in London, New York City, and California, a movie—a big one—was the natural next step. A motion picture comeback with all the bells and whistles could be one ticket to regaining her celluloid stardom.

Meanwhile, movie studios were scrambling to combat the growing threat of television. Studio bosses developed new technologies, even resorting to gimmicks, to pry Americans off their sofas and back into movie theaters. Concurrently, the government required the major studios—Paramount; Loew's Incorporated (the parent company of Metro-Goldwyn-Mayer); RKO; Twentieth Century Fox; Warner Bros.; Universal; Columbia; and United Artists—to divest themselves of their movie theater chains, in order to break up a monopoly as a result of the landmark antitrust case *United States v. Paramount Pictures, Inc.*, 334 US 131 (1948). The sale of the theater chains meant the studios no longer were obliged to create product to fill screens fifty-two weeks a year, nor did they need to keep a stable of stars under long-term contract. The antitrust case, along with the popularity of television, was the beginning of the demise of the Hollywood studio system.

Jack L. Warner, as head of production at Warner Bros., was looking for a surefire hit in an uncertain period after the sale of the Warner theater circuit and as cinematic innovations were developed to enhance the moviegoing experience. 3-D required special glasses to experience its leap-off-the-screen surprises. Cinerama was a widescreen process utilizing three 35mm projectors simultaneously creating one enormous image for a very wide and curved screen.

CinemaScope was a widescreen process without the expense of Cinerama. Television was basic and couldn't offer such novelties, but it was free and right there in the living room. Jack L. Warner was ready to invest some funds from the theater divestiture to expand CinemaScope and Technicolor. A musical film with Stereophonic sound would be a bonus, but a comeback for an undisputed movie star of the first magnitude, Judy Garland, in a tried-and-tested property, *A Star Is Born*, appeared ideal. That was the opportunity Garland needed—a splashy, all-stops-out showcase. Sid Luft, a gambler at heart, needed to prove himself as well. Luft and Garland presented the idea to Jack L. Warner as a package deal, as they already had secured certain rights to the 1937 film version. Warner himself had seen Garland in concert at the Los Angeles Philharmonic Auditorium in 1952 and saw firsthand that she could bewitch capacity audiences with her talent and megawatt star persona.

> The script made the character of Esther Blodgett a singer instead of a fledgling actress, to take advantage of Judy's talents.

Garland and Luft carefully assembled a superlative team of colleagues to reimagine *A Star Is Born* out of its 1937 progenitor. Garland, a former top star of unmatched talent, also brought a lot of baggage onto the studio lot: a fragile constitution, dependency on prescription medication, habits of lateness and volatility, and unmanaged manic depression. She maintained that *A Star Is Born* couldn't merely be very good; it had to be the greatest film of her career. The script, by Moss Hart, was based on the 1937 film screenplay by Dorothy Parker, Alan Campbell, and Robert Carson (from the Academy Award–winning original story by William A. Wellman and Robert Carson). Hart's script is not a facsimile of the 1937 version but rather an improvement on the original; still, it embraces complete sequences from the original that Hart wisely concluded simply couldn't be further enhanced.

The movie's scenario, so unsettlingly comparable to Judy's own backstory, is a meta–"Hollywood on Hollywood" tale: the consequences of the ascent of a new star, while her mentor, a major player in the movies, falls into decline and self-destruction. The script made the character of Esther Blodgett a singer instead of a fledgling actress, to take advantage of Judy's talents. However, much of the plot remains the same as it was in 1937: Norman Maine meets Esther Blodgett and helps establish her film career as the renamed Vicki Lester. They ultimately marry and her professional career soars while his falters due to his severe addiction to alcohol. She plans to leave her career to save him, but he commits suicide to save her. At a Hollywood event shortly after his death by suicide, she memorably introduces herself not as Vicki Lester but as "Mrs. Norman Maine."

Judy persuaded Harold Arlen and Ira Gershwin to compose the film's unforgettable music and lyrics, including "The Man That Got Away," which became one of Garland's signature songs. However, the film's production was beset with troubles, fueling the Hollywood pessimists who maintained that it was doomed from the start. Jack L. Warner experimented with various technological enhancements early in the film's production before selecting CinemaScope and Eastmancolor, which proved costly. Garland's ongoing personal problems caused delays as well, escalating the film's negative cost to $5,019,770 (not including distribution and promotion costs). Garland came close to admitting culpability for these overruns in an article published in 1957: "I'd be the last to deny the picture took an awful lot of time and went way

> The crowds who mobbed the Pantages Theatre to be near the event were estimated to be over twenty thousand strong.

over the budget. But there was a reason for all that. I'm a perfectionist; George Cukor, who directed, is a perfectionist; and so is Sid. We have to have it right; and to make it right took time. It was right too. It was a good picture—as good as we'd hoped it would be."[1]

A Star Is Born premiered at the RKO Pantages Theatre in Hollywood on September 29, 1954. The three-hour film—the second-most-expensive Hollywood production at that time, after David O. Selznick's *Duel in the Sun* (1946)—drew an audience of more than 250 stars, including Gary Cooper, Joan Crawford, Clark Gable, Humphrey Bogart, Lauren Bacall, Marlene Dietrich, Lucille Ball, Desi Arnaz, Elizabeth Taylor, Doris Day, and James Dean. Warner Bros. lavished on *A Star Is Born* the biggest advertising and marketing launch in their studio history. They even touted the production's expense ("$6,000,000 and 2½ Years to Make It!") as part of their campaign.[2]

The crowds who mobbed the Pantages Theatre to be near the event were estimated to be over twenty thousand strong. In addition to a dozen radio stations, KTTV television broadcast the festivities live in Los Angeles as a half-hour local television special with a portion of the telecast aired on NBC national television on the New York City–based *The Tonight Show*. After the premiere, Jack L. Warner hosted a lavish party at the famous Cocoanut Grove nightclub at the Ambassador Hotel.

The reviews were laudatory toward Garland, and the film as a whole won virtually unanimous praise. Those who saw the original, uncut film were mesmerized. The film grossed nearly $700,000 at only seventeen theaters in its first week of release, a figure industry trade paper *Variety* described as "A showing a little short of phenomenal" and described the film's commercial potential as "Boffola box office, period. It will not only mop up as a commercial entry [but] sets a number of artistic standards. Fort Knox, move over."[3] *Life* magazine declared, "*A Star Is Born*, the year's most worrisome movie, has turned out to be one of its best....A brilliantly staged, scored, and photographed film, was worth all the effort....But principal credit for *A Star Is Born* unquestionably goes to imaginative, tireless, talented Judy herself."[4] *Time* proclaimed that Judy "gives what is just about the greatest one-woman show in modern movie history."[5]

Garland had accomplished a miraculous feat. She rose like a phoenix from the ashes of her failed movie career of just four years earlier and produced a masterpiece. However, like the story, *A Star Is Born* the film was to end up as the Hollywood story without a happy ending.

Two weeks after the premiere, Harry Warner, Jack L. Warner's elder brother and president of Warner Bros. Pictures, decreed the film was too long and had to be cut by over thirty minutes from the original 181-minute running time to placate exhibitor demand for a shorter film. Although *Gone With the Wind* (1939) had been reissued in 1954 at 220 minutes (not including intermission) and proved one of the top-grossing films that summer, Benjamin Kalmenson, president of Warner Bros. distribution, dismissed this precedent and ordered *A Star Is Born* cut down to 154 minutes. The press and public condemned the decision. The film's revenues and positive word of mouth quickly evaporated. The unique motion picture experience created by George Cukor and Judy Garland suddenly became a deeply unsatisfactory one. "*A Star* Is Shorn" headlined *New York Times* film critic Bosley Crowther's 1954 assessment of the shortened version. Crowther lamented, "…virtually every cut in the picture leaves a gaping and baffling hole, so that not only the emotional pattern but the very sense of the thing is shorn."[6]

Garland's subsequent loss of the Best Actress Academy Award is still regarded as one of the greatest upsets in the history of the Oscars. Despite the superb showcase of her talent and the verisimilitude of her performance, Garland lost to Grace Kelly in *The Country Girl* (1954). The Academy's rebuke of Garland and the film itself is demonstrated in the fact that out of the six categories in which it was nominated, including Best Actor, Best Actress, Art Direction, Costume Design, Music Score, and Song ("The Man That Got Away"), *A Star Is Born* didn't win a single award. The dismissal of her film by the Academy and the film's commercial failure meant the cancellation of her production company's multipicture deal with Warner Bros. Sadly, and almost incomprehensibly, given the positive critical and public reaction to the original cut of the film, *A Star Is Born* effectively ended Garland's career as a major movie star. After *A Star Is Born*, she was forced to return to concerts and began to perform on television to earn a living and appeared in only a handful of films thereafter.

In 1982, the Academy of Motion Picture Arts and Sciences, through its Academy Foundation, spearheaded the reconstruction (a full restoration was not possible as all the footage could not be found) of the full-length version of the film. A new version was assembled using still photograph montages animating the missing footage with the whole original soundtrack running 176 minutes. Warner Bros., working with the Academy, supported this work and their involvement with the film's reconstruction extended to supporting a tour of the new version in six major cities. The world premiere was held before a capacity crowd at Radio City Music Hall in New York City on July 7, 1983, and enjoyed a clamor of critical and popular acclaim.

Ronald Haver, head of the film department at the Los Angeles County Museum of Art, undertook the reconstruction work as his personal mission. Everyone who admires the film is in his debt and are fortunate also to have his written history of the making and reconstruction of the film—published in 1988—from which this book draws inspiration. As a result of Haver's work and the Academy's promotion, what was once a mutilated motion picture has now become an undisputed masterpiece. The fact that the Library of Congress selected *A Star Is Born* for the National Film Registry of "culturally, historically, or aesthetically significant" films in 2000 supports this assertion. In 2010, Warner Bros. scanned the film's original camera negative at 6K resolution for preservation purposes and tweaked the 1983 reconstruction to achieve the highest possible visual and aural quality. The first Turner Classic Movies Film Festival gave this enhanced, digital version of *A Star Is Born* a world premiere on April 22, 2010, with Lorna introducing her parents' film. In a life and career filled with "comebacks," it is only appropriate that Garland's film continually reemerges to recapture the interest of the moviegoing public.

As complicated as its star, *A Star Is Born* remains a dazzling rendition of an old Hollywood tale. The latest remake, in 2018, starring Stefani Germanotta (Lady Gaga) and directed by, costarring, and coproduced by Bradley Cooper, demonstrates the enduring appeal of this story as it entertains a new generation of filmgoers.

—JEFFREY VANCE, LOS ANGELES, 2018

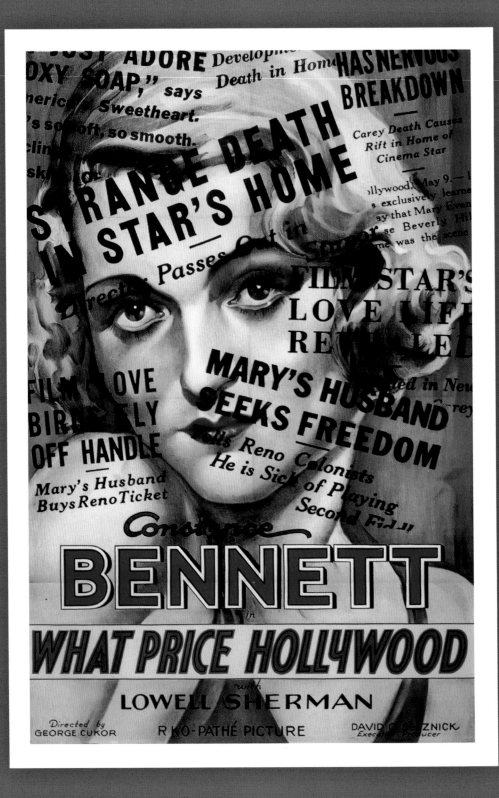

Chapter One

BEGINNINGS:

WHAT PRICE HOLLYWOOD? (1932)

AND *A STAR IS BORN* (1937)

SEVENTEEN YEARS BEFORE JUDY GARLAND MADE CINEMA HISTORY IN Warner Bros.' *A Star Is Born* (1954), David O. Selznick produced the first film of that famed title. But the story doesn't start there. The roots of the 1937 version lie in yet another film with a similar plot, an early pet project of Selznick's titled *What Price Hollywood?* (1932). A tragic love story with the glamour of Hollywood as its backdrop, the film is a Depression-era Cinderella tale with a dark undercurrent that explores the emptiness of celebrity. As one Hollywood star ascends, another great talent declines, and the story climaxes with a suicide. It established the archetype for the classic Tinseltown rise-and-fall tale, and was the first truly noteworthy film by the esteemed director George Cukor.

What Price Hollywood? is the end result of a complicated evolutionary process. In 1932, Selznick purchased a juicy yarn by Hollywood journalist and screenwriter Adela Rogers St. Johns called *The Truth About Hollywood*. Playwright and screenwriter Jane Murfin further

OPPOSITE: One-sheet poster from *What Price Hollywood?* (1932).

developed this original treatment, after which Ben Markson adapted it into a screenplay that was later revised by journalist and screenwriter Gene Fowler and Rowland Brown. Rewrites, and uncredited contributions from Robert Presnell Sr., Roger Stevens, and Allen Rivkin resulted in the screenplay that producer Pandro S. Berman and executive producer David O. Selznick approved, and George Cukor agreed to direct for RKO Pathé.

A succession of working titles for the script matched its string of writers: *The Truth About Hollywood, Hollywood Madness,* and *Hollywood Merry-Go-Round* were all considered but ultimately rejected. The film's final, definitive title is a reference to the famous 1924 anti-war play *What Price Glory?* by Maxwell Anderson and Laurence Stallings that had been made into a popular film in 1926. Selznick selected glamorous blonde Constance Bennett for the lead role of Mary Evans, with actor-director Lowell Sherman playing opposite her as film director Max Carey. Neil Hamilton as romantic interest Lonny Borden and Gregory Ratoff as producer Julius Saxe (a character modeled after movie mogul Samuel Goldwyn) filled out the key supporting roles.

George Cukor, who had codirected his first film, *Grumpy* (1930), just two years earlier, was a veteran of the New York theater world and served an apprenticeship as "dialogue director" during the transition period from silent pictures to "talkies," most notably for Lewis Milestone's *All Quiet on the Western Front* (1930). His stage experience resulted in a well-deserved reputation as a superb director of actors. Cukor adored performers and performing. Telling stories about actors was to be a common thread in his work and would inform *A Star Is Born.* Though it was an integral launching pad for Cukor's career, *What Price Hollywood?* was Selznick's passion project. The producer guaranteed his film's success not only with a fine cast and a sympathetic director, but also with rich black-and-white cinematography by the doyen of Hollywood cameramen, Charles Rosher, excellent settings imagined by art director Carroll Clark, and a striking musical score by composer Max Steiner.

What Price Hollywood? opens on Bennett's Mary Evans primping for her evening shift as a waitress at the famous Brown Derby restaurant, where the Hollywood elite dine. A movie magazine has informed her which silk stockings to slide on, which dress to don, and which lipstick to select, and how to apply it. In a memorable visual introduction to Mary's fantasy world, she holds up a page featuring an image of Greta Garbo and Clark Gable, and, imitating Garbo, plays a miniature love scene with her magazine idol Gable. Judy Garland, a few years later, would recall this scene by singing "You Made Me Love You" to a scrapbook full of Gable pictures in *Broadway Melody of 1938* (1937), creating a pivotal moment in her early career.

Mary is a young, pretty Hollywood hopeful, but not an innocent. She trades on her guile and her beauty, wringing the most out of every opportunity to place herself squarely in the sights of the producers and directors who frequent the Brown Derby. Mary is ready to be discovered—curled, lashed, and peroxided—but unconcerned with the work and the commitment that must follow the superficial powder and polish. She sets her sights on director Max Carey, in top hat and tails, who stumbles into the restaurant one evening, inebriated but endearing. Mary sidles up to his table, stars in her eyes, schemes in her head, and charms the director.

Carey is momentarily taken with Mary; he invites her to leave her job at the bowler-shaped restaurant to attend the premiere of his latest celluloid triumph at Grauman's Chinese Theatre in Hollywood. At the event, she matches him move for move, line for line, and while wearing just street clothes and arriving in a dilapidated Ford Model T, she affects the air and accent of British nobility to impress the crowd and the radio audience, then swans into the theater with a hearty laugh. The next morning, in his own bed and hung over, Carey remembers nothing of the night before, while Mary, who has slept on his sofa, is credited with getting him home safe and fairly sound. Carey admires Mary's moxie. When she plainly states that all she needs is a break, he instructs her to be on his set the next day for a bit part in his current production.

Stage ten is a crush of snaking cables, stage-light floor lamps, and the buzz of cast and crew at work on a movie called *Purple Flame*. Carey snags Mary, positioning her on the grand staircase, and gives her an easy line of dialogue as the minor character of Rosemarie: "Hello, Buzzy. You haven't proposed to me yet tonight." However, Mary, untrained and nervous, is unexpectedly awkward in her delivery and unable to take direction, showing not a trace of the

star quality and assurance she displayed when they first met. Carey instructs his assistant director to find a replacement. Apparently, there have been many such tryouts of his late night "discoveries," as producer Julius Saxe (Gregory Ratoff) is all too aware. Max and Saxe are great friends as well as colleagues; the producer is also wise to the fact that his director is a barely functioning alcoholic.

But plucky Mary doesn't give up. She rehearses on the stairs of her boardinghouse, up and down, speaking the line in every mode her inexperience will allow, until an inner light flashes. She uncovers the walk, the talk, and the manner of the character, and peppers Max with telephone calls pleading for another chance. Styled with Marcelled hair and a slinky gown, she is tested, and the footage is rushed to the screening room for Saxe to view. Mary steals a peek from the projection booth, then overhears dialogue uttered in countless subsequent show business tales: "Terrific!" "Who is that gorgeous creature?" "She's a great discovery!" "Where is that girl?

Mary Evans (Constance Bennett) is an aspiring actress given direction by Max Carey (Lowell Sherman) in a scene from *What Price Hollywood?* (1932).

26

Find her and bring her back immediately!" She is offered a long-term contract and, encountering Max, cries, "Mr. Carey, I'm in pictures!"

Publicized as "America's Pal"—an obvious reference to silent superstar Mary Pickford's well-known sobriquet "America's Sweetheart"—Mary's ascent to stardom is capsulized in a brief but breathless sequence, with searchlights sweeping the sky as her image grows to fill the screen. The 1954 version of *A Star Is Born*, by contrast, mirrors Garland's star status by showing the audience what the excitement is based on: the astonishing talents of Esther Blodgett and her alter ego, Vicki Lester. What we see of Mary Evans (no name change) is the filming, after she is an established star, of her singing prettily *"Parlez-moi d'amour"* on a French cabaret set for director Carey. Max himself is suggested to be in a downward spiral. Suddenly, he appears less focused, less in command, more subject to demon drink and personal despair. The axiom for the physics of Hollywood is set: For every rising star, there is one in free fall.

The film was produced during the so-called Hollywood "Pre-Code" era, before the industry hired William H. Hays to preside over and strictly enforce the Motion Picture

---

The film was produced during the so-called Hollywood "Pre-Code" era, before the industry hired William H. Hays to preside over and strictly enforce the Motion Picture Production Code in 1934, and vigilantly remove suggestive situations and risqué dialogue from the American screen.

Production Code in 1934, and vigilantly remove suggestive situations and risqué dialogue from the American screen. A typical example of edgy dialogue of this period is delivered by Carey, on things that will not last: "My liver and a movie star's marriage." Later, with the Hays Code (the popular name for the Production Code) in place, filmmakers scaled back the racy dialogue for *A Star Is Born* (1937). The story was sanitized even more for the 1954 version, in which sexuality is sublimated due to Judy Garland's fluctuating weight and her somewhat androgynous screen presence.

The character of Lonny Borden, the millionaire playboy of *What Price Hollywood?*, is eliminated from future versions of this tale. He and Mary meet at the Santa Barbara Polo Club and later fall in love, a plotline the subsequent films axe in favor of the romance with Norman Maine. Lonny and Mary dine, dance, fall in love, then marry in a super-charged, publicity-seeking ceremony. On the steps of the Hollywood United Methodist Church, Mary Evans is fiercely mobbed, her bridal gown ending up in tatters. The scene is reinterpreted, in both 1937 and 1954 film versions, into the funeral of Norman Maine; on the chapel steps, the widow's black veil is torn away as a souvenir, inspired by the experience of widow Norma Shearer at the 1936 funeral of her husband, producer Irving G. Thalberg.

The rushed romance adds an element of sex to *What Price Hollywood?* but the true love story at the heart of the film is the tale of Mary and Max: starlet and mentor, friends, colleagues, little sister and big brother. They are an entertaining, platonic duo. Selznick and Cukor based Lowell Sherman's character on silent-film director Marshall A. Neilan and the great John Barrymore. (Sherman himself was a director and a drinker who died at age forty-nine, two years after the release of *What Price Hollywood?*) As played by Sherman, Max Carey is dashing and impulsive, witty and urbane, well dressed, with a sophisticated sexual ambiguity. Constance Bennett, who had started her career in flapper-type roles of the 1920s, was transitioning into a screen sophisticate of the 1930s. The part of Mary Evans allowed Bennett not only to wear her costumes well, but to display both her comedic and dramatic skills, further establishing her as the embodiment of the soigné, witty modern woman.

Cukor quickly had become identified with film properties featuring strong female leads (*Tarnished Lady*, with Tallulah Bankhead and *Girls about Town*, with Kay Francis, both in 1931). Apart from the dexterity with which he handles Bennett's scenes, his work on *What Price Hollywood?* demonstrates traces of the high polish of his later pictures.

The film's imagery, especially that which takes Mary Evans from starlet to star, when her glamour portrait, small at first, is propelled forward into a montage culminating in applause, is striking. The montage—one of several filled with kinetic editing, dissolves, and optical effects—was the work of visual effects specialists Slavko Vorkapich and Lloyd Knechtel. Another notable montage is Max Carey's screen suicide. Max's death scene is particularly memorable for the director's choices to employ quick cuts of shots reliving his life in flashes, exaggerated sound effects, and slow motion when Max collapses to the floor. It is an early, unforgettable, slow-motion death in a Hollywood movie, predating by decades the balletic massacre in *Bonnie and Clyde* (1967) and Sam Peckinpah's slow-motion slaughter in *The Wild Bunch* (1969). Before Carey turns his gun to his own chest, there is an exceptional sequence of flashbacks set amid swirling rings of clouds. Accompanying this mental break is a buzz of sound, like a swarm of bees,

FROM LEFT: the director Max Carey (Lowell Sherman), millionaire playboy Lonny Borden (Neil Hamilton), and screen star Mary Evans (Constance Bennett) in a scene from *What Price Hollywood?* (1932).

and yet not quite. The total effect is mesmerizing—an unusually expressionistic gesture in a mainstream film. The remakes of 1937 and 1954 deal with the suicide in a far less brutal manner, the latter backed up with a Judy Garland ballad.

What Price Hollywood? was nominated for one Academy Award: Adela Rogers St. Johns and Jane Murfin were singled out for Best Writing (Original Story), but lost to the renowned screenwriter Frances Marion for King Vidor's *The Champ* (1931). In the film realization of St. Johns and Murfin's tale, Hollywood is presented as a haven of craft at times approaching artistry, and a disciplined industry, as David O. Selznick would have it. It's also a business, its bottom line a monster that can destroy every aspiration. It can devour piece by piece its seasoned professionals, and swallow whole its starry-eyed neophytes. Max Carey lost himself. Mary Evans bought in. In the end, Hollywood always wins.

Selznick made the film on a budget of $416,000 and it earned $571,000, but lost money at the box office ($50,000) as it failed to recover print and advertising expenses during distribution and received mixed reviews despite a compelling story that expertly weaves the comic and tragic, Cukor's sophisticated direction, and fine performances. According to Selznick, who left RKO in 1933 to strike out as an independent producer, *A Star Is Born* was inspired and formed by *What Price Hollywood?*[1] He believed the screenplay for *What Price Hollywood?* didn't live up to the full potential of its subject, and for this reason Selznick revisited the material for *A Star Is Born* five years later.

＞ ・ ＜

IN SELZNICK'S REIMAGINING OF *WHAT PRICE HOLLYWOOD?* **CAUSED A MUCH** bigger stir in Hollywood than its predecessor. *A Star Is Born* (1937) is more glamorous, more expansive, up-to-date, and shot in the early three-color Technicolor process. In her review of the film, titled "*Star Is Born* Shows Hollywood as It Is," gossip columnist Louella O. Parsons recommended her readers to "…lose no time in going to see this delightful human interest drama. Somehow it has completely captured the mood of this business of motion pictures, and two of our most experienced and delightful players, Janet Gaynor and Fredric March, do much to make Mr. Selznick's dream of presenting the real Hollywood via the screen come true."[2]

A few expository scenes into this drama, a dewy girl from North Dakota, Esther Blodgett, arrives in Los Angeles, and, suitcase still in hand, makes her way to Hollywood Boulevard and Grauman's Chinese Theatre, where—even as early as 1937—the famous

---

". . . Somehow it has completely captured the mood of this business of motion pictures, and two of our most experienced and delightful players, Janet Gaynor and Fredric March, do much to make Mr. Selznick's dream of presenting the real Hollywood via the screen come true."

---

forecourt is a must-see for tourists. She marvels at the star power at her feet, especially when she pauses above the foot and handprints of matinee idol Norman Maine, her first "encounter" with him. Esther's daydreams now have a literal, concrete foundation, even though her heart is still in the clouds. Back home in the rustic nowhere, she declared to her family, "I'm going out and have a real life! I'm going to be somebody!" Her sympathetic Grandmother Lettie (May Robson) funds her granddaughter's venture with money she had saved for her own funeral.

The cruel reality of daily life in Hollywood quickly challenges Esther's dreams of stardom. Her room at the Oleander Arms will cost her $6 a week, and at Central Casting, she is bluntly but gently informed that her chances of making a living in the movies are 1 in 100,000. Esther doesn't hesitate to defend herself: "But maybe I'm that one." Janet Gaynor's Esther has a forceful inner confidence and strength that propel her. Constance Bennett as Mary Evans represented beauty meeting up with opportunity. Judy Garland's 1950s Esther would be a far less ambitious young woman, grateful that she is paid to sing anywhere, possessed of a voice that is greater than she knows. Gaynor's heroine, however, has little raw talent, but a fierce determination to succeed.

Gaynor had won the hearts of moviegoers in the late silent era, her sweet, unassuming charm filling the gap Mary Pickford left when she outgrew youthful roles. By the 1930s, Janet Gaynor was shorthand for "girl-next-door," yet she also was an Academy Award–winning star; she had won the first-ever Best Actress Academy Award in 1929 for her portrayals in two Frank Borzage films—*7th Heaven* (1927) and *Street Angel* (1928)—as well as F. W. Murnau's *Sunrise* (1927). She was a logical Esther for Depression-era audiences to embrace. Furthermore, William A. Wellman had just directed her the year before in *Small Town Girl* (1936), and he was helming *A Star Is Born*.

With fellow tenant and friend Danny McGuire (Andy Devine), an assistant director, Esther attends a concert at the Hollywood Bowl, where several rows ahead, an inebriated Norman Maine (Fredric March) confronts a surly press photographer loudly and physically. Esther is alarmed, but a small smile overrides any judgment in her second encounter with Maine. Esther's cash on hand dwindling, Danny hustles up for her a one-night assignment as a server at a Hollywood party. Balancing a silver tray of hors d'oeuvres, she seeks attention by mimicking Garbo, Katharine Hepburn, and Mae West for the unimpressed guests. (Mary Evans also imitated Garbo in *What Price Hollywood?*) The appearance of Norman Maine, fueled by scotch and soda, throws Esther out of her imaginary spotlight in her third encounter with the famous film star. He follows Esther into the kitchen for more of her innocent chatter. Instead, clatter ensues as he drops a plate, then another, and then takes a platter to the head, courtesy of the date he abandoned. However, Esther is still giving Norman the benefit of the doubt as they escape together, hand in hand, out the back door.

At the Oleander Arms, Wellman lines up an unusual and beautiful shot. Framed in the crook of Maine's arm, Esther's face is half in shadow, her visible eye admiring him. Then as

OPPOSITE: One-sheet poster from *A Star Is Born* (1937).

he turns to go—perhaps surprised that the evening has ended without his making a pass—he pauses and utters the famous line that resurfaces in the next two films, "Mind if I take just one more look?"

Maine pesters studio head Oliver Niles (Adolphe Menjou) in the middle of the night, insisting on a screen test for his new discovery. Niles rewards the impressive test (that the audience never sees) with a contract and a new name: the tossed-off "Vicki Lester," a spin on her first and middle names, Esther Victoria. Matt Libby (Lionel Stander), the studio press agent, creates a new biography to suit her new name and image, and Esther undergoes a cookie-cutter transformation in the form of a makeover and posture and elocution lessons. Libby is excellent at his work, a profession that forces him to clean up after Norman Maine, who is in decline and a publicist's nightmare.

Esther's fourth encounter with Norman Maine plays out in the studio commissary, some time having passed, when Norman spies Esther across the counter rehearsing a bit part to herself. Setting his hangover aside, he "reintroduces" himself, and is taken anew with her simple charms. A lightbulb almost appears over his head as he realizes she is exactly the girl the studio has been trying, and failing, to find to play opposite him in his next picture. In the 1954 *A Star Is Born*, Esther/Vicki is a musical singing star whose career doesn't cross over with Norman's; their careers diverge as their lives intertwine. Here, the two are career contemporaries.

There were other major alterations made to fashion *A Star Is Born* out of *What Price Hollywood?* Selznick changed names and added new characters to update the narrative. Matt Libby serves as an antihero for Maine to have an actual antagonist, while Grandmother Lettie is a voice of encouragement to open and close the film. The character of Danny McGuire is blended in as a friend for Esther. Max Carey, the noted director and alcoholic, becomes Norman Maine, the famous actor and alcoholic; Maine is truly a womanizer, while Carey's exploits with women are merely rumor. The plot change necessitated the elimination of Lonny Borden. Mary Evans keeps

OPPOSITE: Star Janet Gaynor, director and cowriter of the original story William A. Wellman, and supporting actor Adolphe Menjou confer during production of *A Star Is Born* (1937).

her own name in 1932, but in 1937, Selznick rechristened the character Esther Blodgett/Vicki Lester. The former is a lively blonde, in waiting to be a blonde bombshell in pictures; the latter is just off the farm, a big dreamer in a small package. Studio executive Julius Saxe evolves into studio chief Oliver Niles, a debonair man of the world, and friend to Maine.

Though not technically a direct remake, *A Star Is Born* borrows heavily from *What Price Hollywood?*—so heavily, in fact, that the RKO legal team threatened, at one point, to file a plagiarism lawsuit against Selznick. RKO never commenced legal action, owing in part to Selznick's careful reimagining of the first film. An entire ensemble of writers reconfigured the original into a freshened story, and the characters into a tighter group. In fact, the writers assigned to the script outnumbered the movie's principal players. Dorothy Parker (the full-time wit), Alan Campbell (her part-time husband), and Robert Carson composed the screenplay out of the story by director Wellman and the aforementioned Carson, with inspiration provided by Adela Rogers St. Johns's original story. Other contributors—uncredited—included Selznick himself, Ben Hecht, Rowland Brown, John Lee Mahin, Ring Lardner Jr., and Budd Schulberg.[3]

The final script was quite different in tone and content from *What Price Hollywood?*, offering more details (and an additional twenty minutes in running time) about its heroine's rise to stardom and her troubled courtship and marriage. At the big sneak preview of her screen debut with Norman, the moviegoers are over-the-moon for newborn star Vicki Lester, but just plain over the failing Norman Maine. As they leave the theater, Norman tells Esther, "A star is born!" The after-party, at the Café Trocadero, belongs to Esther/Vicki, since she unintentionally stole the picture from Norman. Out on the terrace, overlooking the Los Angeles nightscape, Maine proclaims to Esther, "It's all yours, from now on you know. You're a *success*. You can have everything in the world you want. I hope it will make you happy." The words are poignant, for happiness has eluded Norman, despite his success. He discourages Esther's declaration of love for him, fearing that his self-destructive nature is beyond salvation.

OPPOSITE: Norman Maine (Fredric March) and Vicki Lester (Janet Gaynor) attend the preview of their new movie in *A Star Is Born* (1937). The film makes Vicki an overnight success while moviegoers lose interest in Norman.

Libby enthuses prematurely about a Hollywood wedding, advancing Esther's nascent career and salvaging Norman's. Norman has proposed to her at a noisy, messy prizefight, the two acknowledging the elephant in the ring: his drinking. Maine quips, "We thought we'd elope, in the conventional manner." However, Libby wants "the biggest elopement this town ever saw."

The scene cuts to a California county courthouse where, with inmates as witnesses, Esther Blodgett and Alfred Hinkel (Norman's birth name) tie the civil knot. However, Libby has tracked them down, angrily accusing Norman of betrayal. Garland, James Mason, and Jack Carson play an almost identical scene in the 1954 version, after a similar civil service. A lakeside honeymoon via trailer is attempted, but whipping up a simple dinner in the jostling vehicle sends Esther and her steak to the floor. A muddy and rutted road strands them completely.

Wellman steered away from any cinematic flourishes in his take—or Selznick's—on fall and rise in Hollywood. Wellman was not an obvious second choice when George Cukor passed on *A Star Is Born*. He was known for directing the Academy Award–winning aviation epic *Wings* (1927), the gangster classic *The Public Enemy* (1931), and the uncompromising Great Depression drama *Wild Boys of the Road* (1933). But the director invested himself in the project, adapting the story with many of his and Carson's ideas from their original story, *It Happened in Hollywood*. In that story, they created a character called Esther Blodgett who dreams of movie stardom and an alcoholic screen star Norman Maine, whose stardom is waning. *It Happened in Hollywood* also featured the scene in which Blodgett wins an Academy Award, and the ending in which Maine commits suicide by drowning himself in the ocean. (Wellman maintained that this was based on silent star John Bowers, who drowned himself in the Pacific and his body washed ashore on Malibu Beach the next day. However, his death occurred after the script was completed.) Wellman also drew on memories with his ex-wife, the former screen star Helene Chadwick, who has a bit part in the film.[4]

Wellman claimed it was Irene Mayer Selznick who convinced her husband to produce the film. She remembered, "*Star Is Born* came about because I nagged and nagged and nagged David—since R.K.O. I said, 'Hollywood—it's all around you—you can't avoid it. *What Price*

Hollywood? came out of that, but it wasn't right. And David kept fellows around on it, and there was a whole pile of stuff. Out of that nagging came a lot of stories."[5]

Production began on October 31, 1936 at the Selznick International Studios in Culver City, and wrapped on December 28, 1936. During a period when Wellman battled severe influenza, Selznick temporarily replaced him with directors Jack Conway and Victor Fleming—yet it is Wellman's picture, typical of his subtle, straightforward, and well-paced style. Wellman's delicate handling of Fredric March is particularly skillful. March came into prominence playing the flamboyant Tony Cavendish (a character based on John Barrymore) in George Cukor's *The Royal Family of Broadway* (1930) and won the Best Actor Academy Award in 1932 for his outstanding work in *Dr. Jekyll and Mr. Hyde* (1931), a role previously associated with Barrymore's bravura performance in a 1920 silent-film version. March continued to make excellent films directed by top directors such as Ernst Lubitsch and Cecil B. DeMille and starred opposite Garbo in *Anna Karenina* (1935). He underplays Norman, giving a performance entirely devoid of histrionics. Indeed, March's performance is arguably the most powerful piece of acting in the film, despite the fact that Janet Gaynor's role was pivotal, the actress playing a part tailored to her talent. Although silent film player John Bowers's death was said to have informed Norman Maine, the best evidence suggests that John Gilbert and John Barrymore were the models for Maine's self-destructive behavior. Cukor visited John Barrymore in a west Los Angeles sanitarium that the actor had admitted himself into to stop drinking. The director attempted to rally the ailing actor with the offer of a good supporting role in his forthcoming film *Camille* (1936). The Barrymore incident made it into the final script of *A Star Is Born* through Cukor's friendship and long association with Selznick.[6]

Leading up to a critical Academy Awards ceremony, Maine sees his star eclipsed by his wife's supernova. He takes joy in her success, but, after losing his contract and close association with Oliver Niles, Norman seeks solace in alcohol and becomes a cautionary tale as he loses his identity (he is sometimes referred to as "Mr. Lester") and sense of purpose. At the awards banquet, Vicki wins for the film *Dream without End,* and in a passage lifted later for

Judy Garland in the 1954 remake, says simply, "Ladies and gentleman, when something like this happens to you—and you try to tell how you feel about it—you find that, out of all the words in the world, there are only two that really mean anything. 'Thank you.' All I can do is to say them from my heart. All I can do is to keep on saying them...."

An inebriated Norman Maine slinks into the ceremony, and staggering to the dais, congratulates his wife on winning "that valuable little piece of bric-a-brac." Digging in further, he suggests that he would like an award for the worst performance of the year, or, better still, three for his last three pictures. Unaware that Esther has approached from behind to help him down the steps, he gestures broadly, accidentally backhanding her in the face. Gasps are audible; instant remorse and humiliation descend upon him as he slumps to the table and slurs, "Can somebody give me a drink?" Once home, Esther's gold statuette lies askew on the floor. As her Grandmother Blodgett had foretold,

Vicki Lester (Janet Gaynor) wins an Academy Award in *A Star Is Born* (1937). Gaynor used her own Best Actress Academy Award statuette, which she won at the first Academy Awards ceremony held in 1929, for this scene.

for every dream of hers that comes true, Esther indeed pays the price in heartbreak.

Fresh from the sanitarium, Maine returns to an old haunt, Santa Anita Park, the thorough-bred racetrack where former studio nemesis Matt Libby perches beside him at the bar. Maine sips his ginger ale as Libby begins to taunt the washed-up idol, "You can live off your wife now. She'll buy you drinks and put up with you, even though nobody else will." Maine loses his cool and takes a wild swing, but Libby connects with a forceful blow to the face. The crowd recognizes the former star. Norman peels himself up off the carpet, onto his barstool—once again humiliated, shaken, alone—and orders up a bottle of scotch. He disappears for four days, until he is appre-hended for drunk and disorderly conduct, crashing an automobile into a tree, resisting arrest, and injuring one of the arresting police officers. At night court with Oliver, Esther pleads for Maine's release and swears to be personally responsible for her husband. Photographers and reporters circle outside the jail to catch the two together for front-page news coverage. It was a raw, ripped-from-the-headlines scenario few motion pictures had ever dared to depict.

At the Maines' beach house, Esther confides to Oliver her plans to leave Hollywood and take Norman far away to live a private life, to start over. Norman is in the next room, ostensibly asleep, but he hears every word ("…there'll be no more Vicki Lester") before Oliver takes his leave. It's near twilight. Norman, clad in a bathrobe and leather sandals, promises Esther he will reform and announces his fresh start will begin with a restorative swim, "I'm going wading out in our front yard." He embraces her, stops at the door, and repeats a request he made at the end of their first meeting, "Mind if I take just one more look?" He has made his decision: his wife's stardom is more important than his own life.

Back in Hollywood, one newspaper headline reads, "NORMAN MAINE'S BODY FOUND OFF MALIBU; EX-STAR PERISHES IN TRAGIC ACCIDENT!" The funeral is mobbed, the fans and press relentless. Esther, veiled, shrieks in grieving fear as a fan tears away the veil, the last vestige of her privacy. She collapses, weeping, as two stellar Hollywood careers are stomped out in the frenzy. This and the following sequence, are Gaynor's moments to dis-play her acting ability, to go deep, and mostly she succeeds. It is earlier in the movie that she falters. She fails to conjure the level of charisma that Vicki Lester supposedly radiates; she errs too far on the side of the everyday, the common, with scarcely a spark of superstar electricity. In the film, she symbolizes the star from humble beginnings, the average girl who becomes the personification of screen magic. But the full realization of that magic wouldn't occur until the face, heart, and voice of Judy Garland forever defined the role.

As Esther is packing up the beach house to leave Hollywood behind and return home, Grandmother Blodgett shows up and immediately takes charge of the situation. She has come to challenge Esther's determination to give up with some determination of her own. With stern wisdom and support, Lettie reminds her granddaughter, "If you get what you want, you have

Even in 1932, let alone 1937, this basic high/low tale was not exactly considered an inventive idea. However, the film relates a touching story that the public embraced as the basic movie-star legend, part comedy and part tragedy —a romantic portrait of behind-the-scenes Hollywood not quite as it is, but how many would like it to be.

to give your heart in exchange." Esther relents and will attend an event described as "A Tribute to Vicki Lester" at Grauman's Chinese Theatre that evening. With her grandmother, Danny, and Oliver in tow, Esther hesitantly greets the crowd, getting by without incident until she, in her final encounter with Norman, looks down to find herself standing over Maine's theater forecourt footprints; the relationship has now come full circle. Esther steels herself, and for the radio audience, gently but forthrightly announces, "Hello, everybody....This is Mrs. Norman Maine." Tears roll down her cheeks, the music swells, and the film ends.

Even in 1932, let alone 1937, this basic high/low tale was not exactly considered an inventive idea. However, the film relates a touching story that the public embraced as the basic movie-star legend, part comedy and part tragedy—a romantic portrait of behind-the-scenes Hollywood not quite as it is, but how many would like it to be. The Selznick International Pictures production, released by United Artists and once again boasting a music score by Max Steiner, was freshly appreciated in the mid-1930s, and proved to be a critical and commercial success.

At the tenth Academy Awards, held in 1938, Hollywood rewarded itself, in a sense. The film was nominated for seven Academy Awards: Best Writing, Screenplay; Best Writing, Original Story; Best Directing; Best Picture; Best Actress; Best Actor; as well as an oddity from the early years, Best Assistant Director. The film won for Best Writing, Original Story, betting again on the durability and flexibility of the classic show-business tale. (The film also received a Special Award, given to cinematographer W. Howard Greene, for his superb Technicolor cinematography.) Although the genesis of the film remains a source of confusion and dispute, it's suggestive that when William A. Wellman and Robert Carson won for their story, Wellman publicly stated the award belonged to Selznick. At the awards ceremony, Wellman offered the statuette to Selznick and said, "Here, you deserve this. You wrote more than I did."[7] Selznick certainly believed he deserved it and the award remains with the Selznick family to this day.[8] For Wellman, it was simply enough to make a film that would rank as one of his top five favorites of the over eighty films he made in his distinguished career.[9]

The 1937 *A Star Is Born* had a production cost of $1.1 million and grossed $2 million in its initial release. It was rereleased to theaters in 1945 by film distributor Film Classics and enjoyed extensive telecasts in the early 1950s—an important point as the film hadn't been out of the memory of movie audiences when Judy Garland embarked upon her version. The quintessential Hollywood drama had been formed, a dark fairy tale of hopes, dreams, heartbreak, and glamour, seasoned with some ugly truths about failed careers, alcoholism, and suicide. In late 1952, this aging melodrama gained some attention, then some traction, when Hollywood buzzed with the notion of updating the story with songs and starring Judy Garland. Suddenly, everything old was new again.

OPPOSITE: Fredric March and Janet Gaynor in a scene from *A Star Is Born* (1937).

Chapter Two

A STAR IS BORN

(1954):

THE FILM THAT GOT AWAY

TO SEE A STAR IS BORN AT THE INAUGURAL TURNER CLASSIC MOVIES CLASSIC Film Festival on April 22, 2010, was one of the great nights of my life. This was the network's first event of this kind, and they chose Mama and *A Star Is Born* to be the opening night gala presentation at the Chinese Theatre. My twenty-seven-year-old son, Jesse, was excited, and my twenty-one-year-old daughter, Vanessa, was emotional as the lights dimmed. I was thrilled to share with them the world premiere of the new digital version of my mother's musical masterpiece. Thanks to digital technology, the ravages of time were removed from the film. It was quite an event for us all. Besides *The Wizard of Oz*, my children had only watched a handful of their grandmother's films. They had heard me speak many times of *A Star Is Born* and my belief that it was Mama's greatest film. On that night, they were finally able to judge for themselves. The capacity crowd, which included my brother Joe, applauded at the end of scenes and cheered their approval at the conclusion of each musical number. At one point, I looked over to Jesse and Vanessa and said, "You understand now?" They nodded. Now they could fully see and appreciate Judy Garland's power. At the end of the film, sobs could be heard

OPPOSITE: One-sheet poster from *A Star Is Born* (1954).

throughout the theater. Despite the fact I had seen the film many times, even I had tears running down my cheeks. Vanessa reacted as I did when I first saw the film—she cried as she witnessed her grandmother's electrifying performance. "I can't believe she did all that," she kept repeating. Alec Baldwin was among the many celebrities in attendance that evening. After the film ended, he made a point of telling me, "Your mother's performance is one of the greatest on film."

For many years, *A Star Is Born* was an upsetting experience for me. The film's story, and its underlying message about fame, hit too close to home. The enthusiastic reaction of my children spurred me to open up the photographs and memories about the film I have carefully kept and privately collected for decades. Now I could watch and discuss the film with a more optimistic outlook. Mama's movie had not only been showcased with glorious results, but in a way, the accolades the film was receiving decades later helped to soothe the pain it had caused me in the past.

This scene still, from the second attempt at filming "The Man That Got Away," has become an iconic image of my mother.

THE YEAR WAS 1970. THE PLACE WAS NEW YORK CITY. I WAS EIGHTEEN YEARS old and living on my own for the first time when I saw my mother's *A Star Is Born*. It was a late-night television broadcast, and I eagerly stayed awake to tune in. Splintered with commercials and all chopped up, the story didn't really make a great deal of sense to me. I saw Mama leaning against a piano in a dark blue dress, exuding glamour and melancholy as she belted out a torch song. I saw her camouflaged in a strawberry-blonde wig and caked with makeup on a studio lot. I saw her onstage channeling her younger self, with long hair and ribbons in a flashback scene.

Then suddenly, she was in a beach house, clowning through "Someone at Last," a song I had never heard. But there, in the living-room set, was all the furniture I had grown up with: the white leather chairs, the Tang dynasty camel, the hand-painted Chinese screens, the Maurice de Vlaminck painting, and the two tall lamps styled as blackamoor art—African men wearing turbans and holding swords. The turbans were lampshades and are racially insensitive today, but the romanticism of antebellum slavery was actually popular at one time! These were the pieces that followed us into every family home, and every house or apartment where my father lived. You see, after the film wrapped, my father, Sid Luft, who produced *A Star Is Born*, told me that he purchased all the furniture from the set at salvage cost (ten cents on the dollar)

ABOVE: The "Someone at Last" production number from *A Star Is Born* (1954). OPPOSITE: Vicki Lester improvises with two palm leaves as she acts out the "Someone at Last" musical number. Photo by Bob Willoughby.

and had it moved into our two-story, five-bedroom, five-bath English Tudor home at 144 South Mapleton Drive in the Los Angeles neighborhood of Holmby Hills. (Jack L. Warner wrote in his autobiography that my father "borrowed" the pieces from the Warner Bros. studios for a party and never returned them. This isn't true. In fact, my father sued Warner over such false claims in his book and settled out of court.) Now the film held a special emotional significance for me. Here was not only my mother, but echoes of my father, and household decor I had grown up with. I grew up on the set of *A Star Is Born*, literally.

I knew my father much longer than I did my mother. I was still sixteen—the age when my mother played Dorothy Gale in *The Wizard of Oz* (1939)—when she died. (My brother, Joe, was fourteen and my elder sister, Liza, was twenty-three and already had a career of her own.) It was incredibly painful for me to watch *A Star Is Born* for the first time. Up until then, I had only seen Mama on-screen as a girl, either in *The Wizard of Oz* or one of her many screen teamings with Mickey Rooney. That girl was a stranger. The person I knew as my mother was right there on television in *A Star Is Born*. I have the same feeling when I watch *Judgment at Nuremberg* (1961), *A Child Is Waiting* (1963), or *I Could Go on Singing* (1963). This was Mama. After that first experience, I would watch *A Star Is Born* once in a while, here and there, without fully understanding the high regard some people expressed for it. It felt scattered, choppy, not the great piece of work I later—much later—came to appreciate. I eventually came to regard it as "the film that got away."

The production's journey starts back in 1951. Sometime before my mother and father became the Lufts, they were enjoying a Sunday drive through Connecticut during her record-breaking nineteen-week engagement at the Palace Theatre on Broadway. In a reflective mood, she recalled viewing, years before, the Janet Gaynor–Fredric March version of *A Star Is Born* (1937) and feeling a remarkable connection to the story of a fated relationship between a talented newcomer on the rise and a matinee idol drinking his way to the bottom, all set within the hurly-burly of Hollywood. She saw that film, at its basic level, as the story of a young woman blossoming under the guidance and nurturing love of an older man. On a

OPPOSITE: A photographer's proof sheet records my first visit to the set of *A Star Is Born*. Photos by Bob Willoughby.

subconscious plane, this must have resonated with Mama because it mirrored the dynamic of her own unresolved relationship with her beloved father. She had proposed a remake, in which she would star, to MGM, but they dismissed her suggestion. They thought her longtime fans would never accept her as the wife of an alcoholic.

Mama had actually played the character of Esther Blodgett in a one-hour broadcast adaptation for the CBS Radio Network anthology series *Lux Radio Theatre*, which aired on December 28, 1942. She acted (but sang no songs) opposite Walter Pidgeon as Norman Maine. When Mama mentioned her dream project, Dad heard opportunity knocking. Some of the screen rights had become available. The original owners, David O. Selznick and John Hay "Jock" Whitney, auctioned off various properties when they dissolved their partnership and Edward L. Alperson now possessed some of these rights when he purchased negatives and prints to *A Star Is Born* and was looking to profit from them. Alperson was a film producer as well as president of Film Classics, a company that reissued older films. My father began negotiations both to secure rights to the original material from Alperson and to arrange a production agreement from Jack Warner of Warner Bros. studios. (Selznick retained some foreign rights to the 1937 *A Star Is Born* and a dispute began between Warner Bros. and Selznick that wasn't settled until 1955, when Selznick traded his remaining rights to the film plus a $25,000 payment to Warner Bros. in exchange for their remake rights to Ernest Hemingway's *A Farewell to Arms*.) Warner was impressed by Mama's recent high-profile "comeback" with sold-out appearances at London's Palladium and the Palace in New York City. She resurrected two-a-day vaudeville (a matinee and evening performance daily) on Broadway and won a special Tony Award in 1952 for her work. However, Warner saw firsthand her artistry at her explosive concerts at the Los Angeles Philharmonic Auditorium. The mogul was confidant of the viability of the deal. He was a gambler, like my father. Both men sensed that the stakes were high and the time was right to take a chance.

This was the early 1950s, the era of the Eisenhower administration. The Red Scare was on everyone's mind, and Hollywood was hit hard by the House Un-American Activities Committee and the demagogue Senator Joseph McCarthy. The motion picture industry was in a state of flux. Fewer people were attending movies, choosing instead to stay home and watch such popular programming as *The Ed Sullivan Show* (1948–1971), *The Jack Benny Program* (1950–1965), and *I Love Lucy* (1951–1957) on television. Cinerama, 3-D, and CinemaScope were gimmicks the movies employed to get people off their sofas and back into movie theaters. *The Robe* (1953) was the first film using the new CinemaScope process. It was no classic, but the size of the screen caused hordes of curious people to line up to see the spectacle. Change was in the air. The major movie studios had recently been forced to divest their theater circuits as a result of a landmark antitrust lawsuit. Though the divestment made a studio like Warner Bros. flush with cash to invest, it marked the beginning of the end of the old Hollywood sys-

This was the early 1950s, the era of the Eisenhower administration. The Red Scare was on everyone's mind, and Hollywood was hit hard by the House Un-American Activities Committee and the demagogue Senator Joseph McCarthy.

tem—the "dream factory" that produced a stable of contracted stars like my mother. Despite all these setbacks, Hollywood was still churning out products we now consider classics. The year *A Star Is Born* was released, it was competing against such heavy hitters as Elia Kazan's *On the Waterfront* (1954) starring Marlon Brando, and Alfred Hitchcock's *Rear Window* (1954), an unforgettable vehicle for James Stewart and Grace Kelly.

Warner Bros. entered into a multipicture contract with my parents' production company, named Transcona Enterprises, in August 1952. *A Star Is Born* would be the first picture out of the gate; rather than a straightforward musical, it would revolve around several musical numbers, all sung by Judy Garland. It was hyped as her big movie comeback, even though she was just thirty years old. Mama's fifteen years at MGM have taken on a tinge of mythology over the years. In 1935, when she was only thirteen, Louis B. Mayer signed her to a long-term contract, though not quite certain what to do with her. He loaned out her services to Twentieth Century Fox for *Pigskin Parade* (1936), figuring on trying her out at no expense to his own studio. Mayer soon decided that having signed both Judy Garland and Deanna Durbin was a mistake; they had one young girl singer too many on the lot. Mama made the cut, while Durbin was picked up by Universal Pictures and became a swift success in Henry Koster's *Three Smart Girls* (1936). Mayer was determined to prove to himself and to the industry that he had made the right choice in keeping Judy. Fortuitously, one of Mama's great champions at the studio was Ida Koverman, Mayer's executive secretary, who was determined to have the young singer's career be a regular topic of discussion by the MGM front office.

It always amazes me that my mother's beauty was not praised and nurtured during her formative years. Mama was gorgeous! I have always wished I resembled her more than my father. But Hollywood didn't appreciate her looks as much as I do. Concerned that she was overweight and unfavorably comparing her appearance to MGM's beautiful, mature female stars like Hedy Lamarr (even referring to Mama as a "little hunchback"), Mayer had studio doctors prescribe Benzedrine to the young, impressionable girl. A highly addictive amphetamine that suppressed appetite, Benzedrine was considered the new wonder drug at the time. Combined with phenobarbital, these stimulants made weight loss easy and doubled your energy. No one at the studio gave much thought to the long-term effects such drugs would have on their personnel. Even my grandmother, Ethel Gumm, voiced no objections. Grandmother made it her job to ensure that Mama obeyed the studio and fulfilled her obligations, for which she handled the finances. Her fee was deducted from her daughter's salary. My grandmother was Momma Rose, the ultimate stage mother of Gypsy Rose Lee, before Arthur Laurents wrote the book and crafted the infamous character for his classic 1959 musical *Gypsy*.

OPPOSITE: Mama was given the surname "Garland" (chosen by vaudeville headliner George Jessel) and called Frances Garland at the time this portrait was taken in Chicago, 1934. She rechristened herself "Judy" (after the contemporary Hoagy Carmichael-Sammy Lerner Song) the following year. Photo by Bloom

While Mama was waiting to be placed in a film, she kept busy learning and rehearsing songs with Roger Edens. My mother adored Edens. He had a deep Southern accent (reminiscent of her father's) and he came into her life at a time when she craved fatherly guidance. He accompanied her on the piano, giving her lessons in phrasing and diction, and honing her natural quick-study skills. He became her protector as well as mentor. It was the best schooling she ever had, far more useful than the education she received in the little classroom on the lot with her fellow pupils Mickey Rooney and Lana Turner. For Clark Gable's thirty-sixth birthday party in 1937, Roger Edens wrote a new verse about Gable as an introduction to the song "You Made Me Love You." Mama debuted the piece for the guests, reminding L. B. Mayer of his neglected prize. The song was inserted into *Broadway Melody of 1938* (1937) as "Dear Mr. Gable (You Made Me Love You)" and became the movie's highlight.

As a result, Mama was slated to appear in two musical comedies in production at the same time: *Thoroughbreds Don't Cry* (1937) with Mickey Rooney and Sophie Tucker, and *Everybody Sing* (1938), with Allan Jones and Fanny Brice. She sang the popular ballad "Zing! Went the Strings of My Heart" (one of her audition pieces for Mayer) in *Listen Darling* (1938), teamed again with her cherished friend Mickey in *Love Finds Andy Hardy* (1938), and barely stopped working at MGM for the next twelve years. In addition to the movies, between 1936 and 1950, she recorded over eighty "sides" for Decca Records, participated in over two hundred radio shows, and made personal appearances to promote her films or entertain American servicemen during World War II. With their perky on-screen chemistry, the Rooney-Garland teaming was perfected in a series of popular "let's put on a show" musicals, the best of which are *Babes in Arms* (1939) and *Girl Crazy* (1943).

"As a performer," Mickey Rooney has said of Mama, "I thought she was the perfect partner. Her sense of timing was flawless....A picture like *Girl Crazy* was hard work but God, we had fun!"[1] It truly was a fun and exciting time for my mother. But the roots of some serious problems were forming. At that time, she was a sport, a team player, but the studio wanted a super-kid, capable of wonders when fatigued, magic when low, and sparkle when driven into overtime. Someone from MGM would arrive at her home at 4:00 a.m. to wash and set her hair as well as apply her makeup. She was driven to work at 6:00 a.m. The early call at home circumvented child labor laws and made the most of her time at the studio. While Rooney enjoyed a hamburger lunch at the studio commissary, Mama was given a bowl of consommé. (Mayer was especially proud of his mother's chicken-matzo ball soup recipe that the studio commissary served every workday, but my mother was only allowed the broth.) She pushed through fifteen-hour days on little sustenance, her star rising higher and higher as the world fell in love with her voice and infectious personality.

The Wizard of Oz, because of its enormous expense, was not a big commercial hit in its original release in August 1939; its status as one of the great movies grew over time with theatrical reissues in 1949 and 1955, its first broadcast on network television in 1956, and later as an annual television event from 1959 to 1998. Although the screen rights were purchased for my mother, Mayer at one point had his sights on the world's biggest child star, the curled and dimpled Shirley Temple, for the lead role of Dorothy Gale. However, a deal could not be struck with Twentieth Century Fox, who had Temple under contract, and the role went back to Mama. A tale she liked to tell of the making

A portrait of Mama as Dorothy Gale with her dog, Toto, from *The Wizard of Oz* (1939). Prior to Victor Fleming assuming the role as the film's director, George Cukor worked on the film for a short period but changed Mama's elaborate hair and makeup to the more natural auburn appearance depicted in this photograph and what is shown in the finished film.

of *The Wizard of Oz* involved Bert Lahr, Ray Bolger, and Jack Haley—better known as the Lion, the Scarecrow, and the Tin Man. The three actors would repeatedly close ranks when skip-hopping down the yellow brick road, leaving Mama to fall in behind. Director Victor Fleming finally had enough and shouted, "*Hold it!* You three dirty hams, let that little girl in there!"[2] Mama's performance is what brought the movie to life, above and beyond all its Technicolor gloss and timeless charm, making it into a must-see for each new generation. She is natural, endearing, and a singer of astonishing maturity, though just sweet sixteen.

Mama placed her hand and foot prints in cement in the forecourt of Grauman's Chinese Theatre in Hollywood on October 10, 1939, prior to the premiere of *Babes in Arms* (1939), with Mickey Rooney accompanying her. The following year, Mickey presented Mama her first and only Academy Award—a Special Award given to juvenile talent—for her outstanding work onscreen in the year 1939. It was a miniature Oscar statuette which she disliked, as it represented her being treated as a child, even though she was nearly eighteen. (I have that statuette now and it's very dear to me. I treasure it, even if Mama didn't.) Nevertheless, these two events

bolstered her status in the film industry. The only downside to *The Wizard of Oz*—and it is significant—is the lifelong price my mother had to pay for pleasing the front office at MGM. Her life was good, it was bad, and it was ugly. The good was the opportunity to have her raw talent and hard work assisted by the greatest team of people in the world

OPPOSITE: The Scarecrow (Ray Bolger), the Tin Man (Jack Haley), Dorothy (Mama), and the Cowardly Lion (Bert Lahr) in a scene from *The Wizard of Oz* (1939). RIGHT: Mama, recipient of a Special Award (Juvenile Award) with Mickey Rooney, presenter, at the twelfth Academy Awards held at the Cocoanut Grove at the Ambassador Hotel in Los Angeles, February 1940.

Mama as Esther Smith in *Meet Me in St. Louis* (1944). The natural integration of the film's musical numbers into the story served as a model for *A Star Is Born*. Her appearance here would be replicated for a scene a decade later in the later film's "Born in a Trunk" sequence, in which Mama plays a teenager. In both instances, the costumes were designed by Irene Sharaff.

and be transformed into a shining star. The bad was being treated as a product, facing constant fatigue, and having no personal life. The ugly? Her abuse of and later dependency on prescription medications, and the ensuing breakdowns these substances helped trigger.

Mama played on; her first over-the-title solo star billing was *For Me and My Gal* (1942), featuring the motion picture debut of Gene Kelly. She splendidly segued into adult roles with that film and with *Presenting Lily Mars* (1943). Her last adolescent role was Esther Smith, the girl next door, in *Meet Me in St. Louis* (1944). This enduring classic was significant both for film history and for my mother, who fell for her director, Vincente Minnelli. An older man as well as a highly skilled artist of great taste, he was just her type. *Meet Me in St. Louis* was also the picture that introduced her to her longtime makeup artist, Dorothy Ponedel, and to costume designer Irene Sharaff. Along with *The Wizard of Oz* and *A Star Is Born*, *Meet Me in St. Louis* is one of the undisputed masterpieces in my mother's filmography. It pleased her more than any film she had made up until that time.

Mama and Vincente wed in 1945, when her divorce from her first husband, bandleader and composer David Rose, was finalized. The Minnellis were a union made in MGM heaven. Although they did not enjoy a private relationship as successful as their working one, they did manage to make two masterpieces together: *Meet Me in St. Louis* and my sister, Liza, born Liza May Minnelli on March 12, 1946. Despite this time of great professional and personal happiness, Mama was becoming notorious for budget-busting delays caused by her tardiness and temperament, the result of her growing dependence on medication as well as her willful behavior. A true actress emerged in *The Clock* (1945) a full-fledged drama that Minnelli directed at her insistence. She reunited with Gene Kelly for *The Pirate* (1948), directed by Minnelli. The production was a difficult one. Mama's unhappiness with the material—fearing that it was not commercial enough—endangered her fragile mental state. The production evolved into a Gene Kelly showcase (what else does anyone remember from the film, other than a scantily clad Kelly in "The Pirate Ballet" sequence?) more so than a Kelly-Garland joint teaming. *The Pirate* led to a major depressive episode. However, she rallied sufficiently to make *Easter Parade* (1948), teaming with the great Fred Astaire and directed by her friend Charles "Chuck" Walters. The plot involved an older vaudevillian as mentor and eventual partner to a much younger performer. It was the old Pygmalion-Galatea tale—shades of her future *A Star Is Born* plot.

Mama's dependency on prescription drugs was the worst-kept secret in Hollywood by 1949. According to my father, her drug use was the source of comment in tabloid publications as well as an investigation by Harry J. Anslinger, the first commissioner of the Federal Bureau of Narcotics and America's first "drug czar." The ghost of drug dependency was always in my mother's home. Everybody was ill-equipped to deal with that part of her story. None of her husbands understood it. MGM didn't understand it, either. No one knew the physical and psychological effects of addiction. They were as much in the dark as my mother. Mama now squirreled pills just as she previously hoarded cookies or candy bars from watchful eyes. She was a childlike person and she didn't want to get caught. She seemed to crank up her own gossip machine. MGM public relations had its hands full keeping the lid on speculation about alleged affairs with bandleader Artie

Shaw, screenwriter-producer (and later director) Joseph L. Mankiewicz, screen heartthrob
Tyrone Power, and the legendary Frank Sinatra. Mama's erratic behavior forced Mayer to
replace her in several projects, most notably
in *Annie Get Your Gun* (1950), a starring role
ultimately played by Betty Hutton. In *Summer Stock* (1950), Gene Kelly partnered with
her as a favor, believing he was indebted to
Mama for her invaluable support in launching his film career.

Summer Stock *was nothing earth-shattering
—a throwback to the type of light romantic musicals she'd done with Mickey Rooney
over a decade earlier, but it contains her show-
stopping "Get Happy" number. Clad in a rak-
ish man's hat and fitted black jacket that reveals
every inch of her gorgeous gams, her lips lac-
quered fire-engine red, Mama brings the house
down with her triumphant rendition of Harold Arlen's gospel-flavored tune. (The sequence
was photographed several weeks after the main
filming was completed in 1950 and after she
lost ten pounds. She looks so different in this
sequence that for many years people speculated

OPPOSITE: Mama films "Get Happy," her final solo
musical number in *Summer Stock* (1950) and her last
completed film for MGM.

that it must have been inserted from an earlier, unreleased Judy Garland film.) "Get Happy" was a high note to end on: *Summer Stock* would be her last film for MGM, despite the film's commercial success. During preproduction of *Royal Wedding* (1951), she was placed on her third and final suspension, replaced by Jane Powell, and her days at the studio were over. Mayer later stated with apparent sincerity, "There has never been any other motion picture star to equal Judy Garland in genius and love of the public. The bitterest moment of my life was when I had to let her go."[3]

It was an equally bitter moment for Mayer's star. Devastated, and feeling isolated after losing her professional home and family, Mama attempted suicide on June 19, 1950, by cutting her throat with a broken edge of a water glass in her bathroom. The gash was not deep at all; she survived to read the next day's headline, "Judy Garland Slashes Throat After Film Row."[4] The news shocked the public and caused an outpouring of sympathy from her fans. Katharine Hepburn, whom my mother held in the highest regard and was a great fan of as an actress, made a surprise visit to my mother's bedside to rally her during this difficult time. Mama never seriously tried to kill herself. Mama's suicide attempts were last-resort methods to gain attention and release anxiety. I believe she felt trapped, misunderstood, and was making a desperate plea for understanding. The act also managed to release her from her contract—which had two years to run and could have prevented her from taking other jobs. She obtained her release from Metro-Goldwyn-Mayer in September 1950. Without MGM resources to shield her, Hollywood's perception of Judy Garland was changing. She was now a deeply troubled celebrity. She had endured electroshock therapy and various hospitalizations. After fifteen years and twenty-nine movies, Mama was suddenly unemployable in the movie business at age twenty-eight, running low on funds, and relying on old friends to see her through. Emotionally, physically, and financially, my mother was spent.

Radio work kept my mother going, but on her slippery slope, even her fragile marriage was now in jeopardy. A legal separation from Vincente Minnelli was in place by Christmas 1950,

OPPOSITE: Mama, attired in her tramp costume to re-create the "A Couple of Swells" number from her famous film *Easter Parade* (1948), made theatrical history with her record-breaking nineteen-week run at the famed Palace Theatre, New York City, during the 1951–1952 Broadway season.

ABOVE: Mama re-creates the "Get Happy" number from *Summer Stock* onstage at the Los Angeles Philharmonic Auditorium, 1952. OPPOSITE: Mama with my father, Sid Luft, at Romanoff's, a popular Beverly Hills restaurant, April 1952.

when Mama made a holiday trip to New York City. There, she encountered Michael Sidney Luft, and a surprising attraction developed. Mama responded to his rugged good looks and personality—so like a character from a Damon Runyon novel and so unlike the refined men she usually favored. A man of many rough edges, and somewhat brash, Sid Luft was a former test pilot, B-picture producer, and gambler with a penchant for the racetrack. He'd already been married twice, and the hard-drinking Humphrey Bogart was his good friend. When he

met Judy Garland, my father saw her as both a lover and an opportunity—a conduit for reflected fame. He fell in love with Judy the person as well as Judy the commodity. For her part, Mama saw Sid Luft as a white knight charging to her rescue, the ideal catalyst to deliver her from the bad times and into a new era. The two married on June 8, 1952, with initial *A Star Is Born* negotiations started. It was an eventful period. They knew Mama was pregnant with me. I was born on November 21, 1952, at 4:17 p.m. by Cesarean section at St. John's Hospital, Santa Monica, weighing six pounds, four ounces. Mama chose "Lorna," from a favorite play—Clifford Odets's 1937 Broadway hit *Golden Boy*, which was made into a popular 1939 movie—and because it would sound nice with "Luft." My father liked it because it was similar to his mother's name, Leonora, and he had a crush in grade school on a classmate named Lorna Doone, after the famous Victorian novel by Richard Doddridge Blackmore. Unlike my elder sister and younger brother, I wasn't given a middle name. Dad's explanation was that I didn't need one. When I asked him about my name as a girl, my father told me that "Lorna Luft" was chosen as it would look great on a marquee. I was a showbiz kid from birth. Shortly after I was born, my mother slid into a postpartum depression.

⇒ • ⇐

THE YEAR 1953 BEGAN IN NEW YORK CITY, WHERE MAMA HAD TRAVELED AS a guest of Jack L. Warner to sing at his daughter's coming-out party. No doubt pleasure was mixed with business while my parents were in Manhattan. Two days later, on January 5, my grandmother, Ethel Gumm, died suddenly in Santa Monica at the age of fifty-nine. Although the two had been estranged at the time of her sudden death, Mama took it hard. They had a contentious relationship for years and she was plagued with guilt and deep sadness.

Mama wasn't down for long. With two partners, Edward L. Alperson (who owned rights to the 1937 *A Star Is Born* production) and Ted Law (a Texas oilman and Dad's partner in a horse stable business called Walfarms), the Lufts formed Transcona Enterprises, holding 75 percent

ABOVE, FROM LEFT: My mother is escorted from the Little Church of the Flowers by my father and Vernon Alves after attending the private funeral service for her mother, Ethel, at Forest Lawn Memorial Park, Glendale, January 1953. Alves was a close friend of my father's and served as associate producer of *A Star Is Born.* • My mother appears with my father at his alimony hearing, 1953. My father had been married previously, to actress Lynn Bari from 1943 to 1950.

interest in the company; Alperson 20 percent; and Law 5 percent interest. An obscure town in Manitoba, Canada, where Dad had often flown with the Royal Canadian Air Force during World War II, provided the company name. Jack Warner invested some of the profits from the sale of the Warner theater circuit and, with Mama's recent concert successes, was about to gamble on *A Star Is Born*, destined to become the most expensive film Warner Bros. had ever undertaken.

Warner Bros. started as a minor studio with four brother/entrepreneurs (Albert, Sam, Harry, and Jack) and the canine Rin Tin Tin as its first star. The studio became a major force in the industry with *The Jazz Singer* (1927) and the advent of "talkies." Warner Bros. was famous for gangster pictures, such as *Little Caesar* (1931) and *The Public Enemy* (1931), and gritty, realistic films like *I Am a Fugitive from a Chain Gang* (1932). The studio later produced some

"[T]he picture had to be the greatest...
it couldn't be merely very good. I had too much at stake...
I had to prove things." —JUDY GARLAND

of the greatest movies of all time, including *The Adventures of Robin Hood* (1938), *Casablanca* (1942), *Now, Voyager* (1942), *Yankee Doodle Dandy* (1942), *Mildred Pierce* (1945), and *The Treasure of the Sierra Madre* (1948), to name just a few.

Warner had experience with independent-minded stars, such as Errol Flynn, Humphrey Bogart, Bette Davis, and James Cagney and recently enjoyed a pleasant and profitable experience with Elia Kazan's *A Streetcar Named Desire* (1951), financed and distributed by Warner Bros. with artistic decisions made by producer Charles K. Feldman and director Kazan. Warner was willing to gamble on Garland.

"[T]he picture had to be the greatest...it couldn't be merely very good. I had too much at stake...I had to prove things," Mama recalled during this period.[5] The financial risk was tremendous, but overriding that was the dream: a comeback in a perfect, tailored-to-fit star part in a major Hollywood movie. Just as important, the deal with Warner Bros. promised her a level of control she had never had before while making a film. My father assured her that she would feel safe, be supported by top talent in the industry, and that she was to make key creative decisions as the film's de facto producer. As Dad had shown at the racetrack, he was a natural gambler. In his eyes, Mama's motion picture comeback was a long shot horse that just might finish in the money.

>= • =<

IN THE MOST UNIVERSAL OF TERMS, *A STAR IS BORN* **IS A HUMAN SEESAW** story of a young woman and a slightly older man. She begins to grow and blossom under his guid-

Jack M. Warner (son of J. L. Warner), Warner Bros. executive Steve Trilling, casting director William Orr, my father, my mother, Jack L. Warner, director George Cukor, and cinematographer Winton Hoch during preproduction.

ance as he withers and fades away. In order to enlarge the basic tale—even beyond its respected 1937 telling—and allow it to sing, Mama (and Dad) turned to friends and former colleagues to work with her once more on the ultimate showcase for Miss Judy Garland.

The consummate Broadway professional, and arbiter of taste, writer/director Moss Hart is best remembered, in collaboration with George S. Kaufman, as the playwright of the immortal theatrical works *You Can't Take It With You* (1936) and *The Man Who Came to Dinner* (1939). The writer had met Mama when she and Minnelli, Hart's great friend, honeymooned in Manhattan in 1945 and she had admired Hart's work, particularly his book and direction for *Lady*

Mama confers with screenwriter Moss Hart and director George Cukor.

in the Dark (composer Kurt Weill's 1941 Broadway musical, with lyrics by Ira Gershwin and starring Gertrude Lawrence). Hart had long been an admirer of Mama's intuitive artistry before the movie camera, a directness that had nothing to do with screen technique. The great English theater actress Ellen Terry described this star quality as that "little something extra" that makes a great star, and Hart quoted this idea in the *A Star Is Born* screenplay to apply to Garland's character. So when my parents presented him with the 1937 script, he didn't need persuading to take on its rewrite. The 1937 Pulitzer Prize–winning playwright and screenwriter for the Best Picture–winning *Gentleman's Agreement* (1947) adapted the script in a swift and expert manner.

Hart remained involved during production, consulting with the film's other major creative force, veteran director George Cukor, who always deferred to Hart when cuts or alterations were needed. The two men had an excellent rapport, which had been formed when Cukor directed *Winged Victory* (1944), based on a play of the same name by Hart, who also wrote the screenplay. The two men had known each other since their Broadway theater days in the 1920s. For his rapid and masterful rewrite, Hart was paid $101,000 (a symbolic sum, granting him $1,000 more than the star of the film).[6]

Hart's expert touch with incident and dialogue yielded a screenplay that hewed closely to the William A. Wellman/Robert

My father's thirty-eighth birthday was celebrated during production on November 2, 1953.

Carson original story of *A Star Is Born*, yet boasted some brilliant resets for the film's first act. Instead of a private party, Esther Blodgett and Norman Maine have their initial electric encounter at "Night of the Stars," an annual glittery benefit gala at Los Angeles's Shrine Auditorium. He is belligerently drunk, about to embarrass himself onstage until rescued by Esther's quick thinking during her performance. Later, backstage, Maine apologizes by commandeering her lipstick to draw on the painted concrete wall: a big valentine heart, pierced with a ragged arrow, that encircles "E.B. + N.M." As he leaves, Esther thinks aloud to Danny McGuire, her friend and piano player, "You know, drunk or not…he's nice." This is a master-class reimagining of the first crossing of the paths of idol and novice.

Hart continues to reinvent as the sleepless Maine goes in search of "the little dark girl" at the famous Cocoanut Grove. He has an exchange with the maître d', who has evidently assisted the actor with similar early-morning hunts. Bruno discreetly indicates a pretty blonde seated with her companion under the droop of a faux palm tree. Maine: "Too young. I had a very young week, last week." Bruno: (pointing out another) "Miss Sheldon? She's very beautiful tonight." Maine: "No. She hit me over the head with a bottle. They only hit me once. The girl in the green dress…" Bruno: "No, Mr. Maine. Pasadena. Leave it alone." That last line has two interpretations. One is that the girl is off-limits: Maine should "Pass-adena," in code. In the other, Bruno is suggesting a type of girl, a virgin from Pasadena, once seen as a haven for "good girls," as opposed to the supposedly looser women one might encounter in den-of-iniquity Hollywood. The dialogue feels authentic, an inside peek at swanky La La Land after hours in the 1950s.

Mama on the stage of the Shrine Auditorium in Los Angeles for the "Gotta Have Me Go with You" number. Actor Tommy Noonan is standing at left.

The Downbeat Club, a boîte on Sunset Boulevard, is another of Hart's inspirations. It is where musicians gather in the wee hours to wind down and riff for each other, and where Bruno believes Maine might find the girl he came looking for. He enters the smoky darkness, hearing Esther's singing voice rising from the depths, accompanied by Danny McGuire on piano and assorted musicians. Maine is jolted by what he hears, mesmerized by a "surge of pleasure," and tells her so at the club and as he drives her home. Esther, surprised by such unvarnished praise, relates her modest girl–singer story in a foreshadowing of the big "Born in a Trunk" sequence. She even speaks of a low point, when she had to work as a waitress—as Mary Evans and Blodgett #1 both did—and how she would never do it again.

Before they part at the Oleander Arms, Norman urges her to remain in Hollywood, promising to get her a screen test. And, in a

"The Man That Got Away" musical number was filmed three times before everyone was pleased with the cinematography, lighting, composition, and costume. The first version was abandoned because it was filmed in standard screen width and Technicolor. This photograph records the second attempt, filmed in Cinema-Scope and Eastmancolor, but the costume (by Mary Ann Nyberg) and hair required further changes. Photo by Sanford Roth.

ABOVE: In a key scene, Norman Maine encourages Esther Blodgett, "A career is a curious thing. Talent isn't always enough. You need a sense of timing—an eye for seeing the turning point—for recognizing the big chance when it comes and grabbing it." Norman believes Esther possesses "that little something extra" required of great talent, which is star quality. OPPOSITE: Three images from the final version of "The Man That Got Away" as it appears in the final version with Mama wearing a costume designed by Jean Louis. Esther demonstrates her "star quality"; Norman Maine observes Esther from a distance; Esther belts out her torch song.

Moss Hart monologue, waxes poetic on the subject of dreams and opportunity. Norman states, "A career is a curious thing. Talent isn't always enough. You need a sense of timing—an eye for seeing the turning point, of recognizing the big chance when it comes along and grabbing it. A career can rest on a trifle, like us sitting here tonight. Or it can turn on somebody seeing something in you that nobody else ever saw and saying, 'You're better than that, you're better than you know.' Don't settle for the little dream. Go on to the big one." The big star and the little singer, so fated to connect, lose track of each other before anything can happen. Esther is forced to work as a carhop at a drive-in, shuttling hamburgers, breaking the vow she had made to herself. Maine locates her in a series of scenes that were considered expendable in the flurry of bad decisions that led to the truncated *A Star Is Born* being put into general release.

A rewarding spin on a scene from the 1937 version is Hart's take on Esther being readied for her screen test. *What Price Hollywood?* and the earlier *Star Is Born* threw the moment away, while Hart revels in a before-and-after studio makeover lampoon. Esther is scrunched

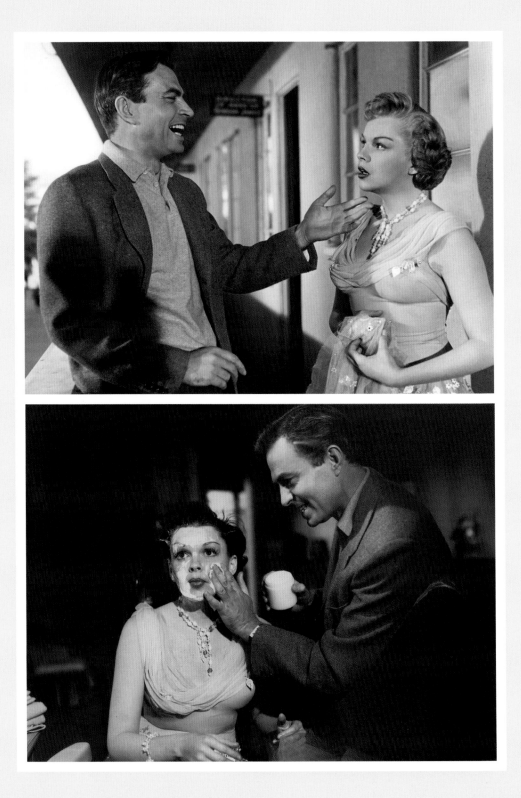

ABOVE: Norman restores the flawed but pretty Esther, and spins her around to look in the mirror at her fresh and lovely brunette self. Esther clutches his hand, leans into his shoulder, seeing herself anew through Norman's eyes. This part of the film had a special meaning to my mother and George Cukor as it echoes their past experience when Cukor worked one week directing *The Wizard of Oz* fifteen years earlier and eliminated the blonde wig and heavy makeup that were preventing my mother from being true to herself and becoming the character of Dorothy Gale. OPPOSITE: Two stills depicting the screen test sequence. AT TOP: Norman laughs at the efforts by the studio makeup department experts to turn Esther into a conventional blonde screen beauty. AT BOTTOM: Norman removes the wig and makeup in order to find the true Esther and encourage her.

in the makeup chair, wrapped in white towels, looking like a deer caught in the headlights, as the experts poke and prod and speak of her as if she weren't there. Next, we see her as a strawberry-blonde glamour gal in a garish pink and purple gown, dripping rhinestones from ears, neck, and bodice, her face an overvarnished kabuki mask. Norman, at first, does not recognize her, then roars with laughter, which sets Esther off. "I've been sitting in that chair since six o'clock this morning!" to which he responds with the quip, "You sat an hour too long, honey." Norman drags her to his bungalow dressing room, where he proceeds to strip away the wig, the putty, and the paint. Esther protests tearfully, parroting the men in the makeup room, "But my nose is very bad, my eyes are all wrong, and my ears are too big… and I…I have no chin." Norman restores the flawed-but-pretty Esther, and spins her around to look in the mirror at her fresh and lovely brunette self. Esther clutches his hand, leans into his shoulder, seeing herself anew through Norman's eyes. She is already in love, and is soon under contract. It's a wonderful scene, and I know it had special meaning to my mother and George Cukor as it echoes their past experience when Cukor worked one week directing *The Wizard of Oz* and eliminated the ridiculous wig and costume that were preventing my mother from being true to herself and becoming Dorothy.

Not satisfied with just that entertaining and moving sequence, Hart conjures up a three-minute playlet, skewering the factory efficiency of Hollywood star-making. Esther ascends the dark stairs to the publicity department, where a Miss Markham (Lotus Robb) palms her off on the wardrobe department, which sends her to the photo department, everyone chiming, "Glad to have you with us." Esther meets the blunt Matt Libby (Jack Carson), the head of the publicity department, who escorts her to a flickering screening room to shake hands with studio chief Oliver Niles (Charles Bickford), who echoes, "Glad to have you with us." He then

ABOVE: Mama and me during production of "The Man That Got Away" sequence. Photo by Sanford Roth. OPPOSITE, TOP: Mama with Jack Carson during production. Carson was a former Warner Bros. contract player who was known for his flair for comedy, even if his best remembered role is in the dark *Mildred Pierce* (1945). Mama had worked with Carson in vaudeville when she was still Baby Gumm of the Gumm Sisters and he was half of the comedy team of Willock and Carson. Mama thought him very funny and great company. OPPOSITE, BOTTOM: James Mason, Jack Carson, Charles Bickford, and Mama enjoy a laugh during production. Of the four main actors of *A Star Is Born*, Bickford was the most reserved. In fact, director Cukor privately referred to Bickford as "Old Ironpants" during production, as he was so serious-minded.

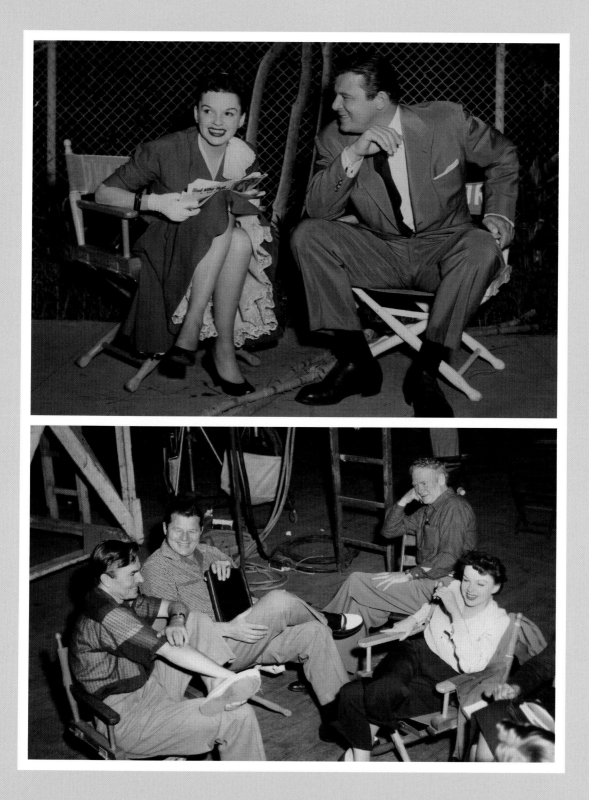

shouts her out of the room as she's blocking the screen. Blinking in the sunlight, she crosses a lofty catwalk with Libby's standard send-off, "We'll have a new name for you by the end of the week." Entering the neighboring building, Esther then reappears and descends the stairs to find herself staring up at the sign for Publicity. She is right back where she started. Next, Esther is a bit player or less, plopped in the seat of a soundstage passenger train car, her arm sleeved in mink, her hand waving a filmy scarf out the window. "Cut!" the assistant director shouts. "We don't want to see your face!" Esther was only cast, it seems, for the use of her hand. She is playing a waiting game.

Norman schemes to put Niles's and Esther's singing voices in close proximity, as the producer has just lost the star of his next musical to a Broadway show. And Niles takes the bait. "Who is that singing?" Norman informs him casually that it's Vicki Lester—and a star is born. The sneak preview of the picture that Niles casts her in, which ends with the show-stopping "Born in a Trunk," the raves it receives from the preview audience, and the pans for Maine's movie which preceded it, close the first act of the original *A Star Is Born*. Moss Hart significantly rewrote the first half of the 1937 screenplay, but the incidents in the second half are largely the same, from the post-preview party to the funeral hysteria. Hart did swap out the prizefight for a studio recording session as the site for the marriage

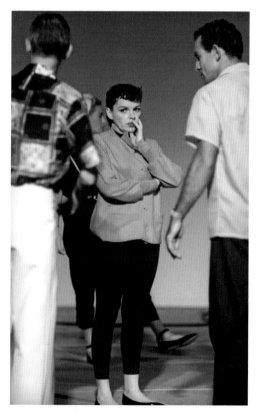

OPPOSITE: Vicki Lester and Norman Maine plan their Malibu dream house. This scene, filmed on location in Laguna, was cut after the film's first preview. Photo by Bob Willoughby. ABOVE: Mama in a pensive moment during a rehearsal.

proposal. He canceled the comical trailer honeymoon in favor of a plain and sentimental motel room. Also gone were the rustic North Dakota scenes and Grandmother Lettie. Both movies end with the heart-wrenching line "This is Mrs. Norman Maine." But Hart envisioned a full-circle finale, with Esther alone on the enormous stage where she and Maine first met, at the same annual charity event, to close the film. There would be, however, no big closing number, no big finish. Judy Garland would not sing audiences out of the theater. Instead, they stuck to the original script.

Hers is the only solo voice heard in the picture, making it a virtual one-woman concert held together by a dramatic narrative.

The gathering of the-best-of-the-best continued as Harold Arlen and Ira Gershwin were signed to provide Mama's songs: Arlen was paid $35,000 for the music and Gershwin $42,500 for the lyrics. Hers is the only solo voice heard in the picture, making it a virtual one-woman concert held together by a dramatic narrative. Moss Hart had outlined the story for Arlen and Gershwin, noting seven suggested scenes for which songs could be written, and the psychological and emotional underpinnings for each. With lyricist E. Y. Harburg, Arlen had composed the score for *The Wizard of Oz*. They were the duo behind the magical "Over the Rainbow," the Academy Award winner for Best Original Song at the Academy Awards held in 1940, which eventually became Mama's signature song. Arlen also composed melodies for what are now referred to as American Songbook classics: "Stormy Weather," "That Old Black Magic," "Come Rain or Come Shine," to name a few. Arlen was certainly one of Mama's favorite composers, and she was sure he could create an entire score just for her—with the right collaborator. That musician would be Ira Gershwin, who gained fame and accolades as his big brother George's lyricist, the two responsible for "I Got Rhythm," "S'Wonderful," and "But

TOP: Mama in a studio recording session with musical director Ray Heindorf. "Working with Garland was just magnificent," Heindorf later recalled. "It was the first time she'd sung in some time, and she was fresh. She knew those songs backward and didn't have to use any music, ever." Photo by Sanford Roth. BOTTOM: Mama recording a musical number. Photo by Sanford Roth.

ABOVE: Vicki Lester acts out a movie scene in the "Someone at Last" musical number. OPPOSITE: Cinematographer Harry Stradling, my mother's original choice as the film's cinematographer, visits Mama during a break in the filming of the "Someone at Last" sequence while hairstylist Helen Young attends to my mother on an adjacent ladder. Photo by Bob Willoughby.

Not for Me." Gershwin worked less after his brother's passing, but did collaborate with Jerome Kern and Kurt Weill for the movies and for Broadway. The same agent, the legendary Irving "Swifty" Lazar, represented Gershwin, Arlen, and Hart; deals were made swiftly, accounting for how Lazar had acquired his nickname. With his help, Mama assembled her first choices from among her good friends and greatest supporters.

With no opening number, the first song is for the Glenn Williams Orchestra, a late-model swing band, and its vocalist Esther Blodgett, with backup from two chorus boys: the catchy

"Gotta Have Me Go With You." The strong patter and rhythm distract Norman Maine from his backstage blunder, drawing him to join, uninvited, into the song and dance. Esther saves Maine, and the day, by cleverly making the sodden star part of the act, ending in a jazz-hand strut that wins laughter and applause from the crowd.

The melodic torch number "The Man That Got Away" is the song most closely identified with *A Star Is Born*. It is modern, urban blues, referred to by Gershwin before it had a title as the "Dive Song" that Esther sings for herself and the band. She is unaware that she is captivating, in the dark, the man she rescued earlier in the evening. The ballad is considered one of the great songs composed for the movies, confounding people who care about such injustices that it lost the Academy Award to Sammy Cahn and Jule Styne for "Three Coins in the Fountain"—a sweet, sentimental favorite, but a banal tune compared to the haunting "The Man That Got Away." The losing song is a powerful lament, a dazzling pop aria in plain clothes, one Mama tucked into with all her vocal variety, drive, and brass. Her interpretation actually displeased the film's vocal arranger and coach, Hugh Martin, who wanted to hear a hushed, smoky, understated rendition, so acutely that he left the film and returned to New York City. Curiously, she had previously collaborated with Hugh Martin on "Have Yourself a Merry Little Christmas," written by Martin and Ralph Blane for *Meet Me in St. Louis,* when she determined the original lyric was too downbeat. Mama insisted on alterations and the song, once altered, went on to become a holiday standard. Here, my mother's instinctive musical delivery drowns out any objections. Her voice seems to express the heartache and regret of every love-affair-gone-bad since the beginning of time. It is a stellar example of her ability to channel the emotions of the masses. "The Man That Got Away" and "Here's What I'm Here For" were released in 1954 by Columbia as 45 rpm and 78 rpm records.

The film score is performed as musical presentations: onstage, in a club, on record or radio, on-screen, in rehearsal, on set. However, the songs still push the story along, without

OPPOSITE, FROM TOP: Mama with Cukor during production of the "Someone at Last" musical number. Photo by Bob Willoughby. • Mama consults with Cukor during a break in the production of the "Someone at Last" sequence. Dance director Richard Barstow leans on the edge of the sofa. Photo by Bob Willoughby.

hitting the nail on the head. One of the Warner Bros. recording soundstages was used for Mama as Esther to lay down a track, with a large orchestra and chorus, for "Here's What I'm Here For," a song for a Vicki Lester movie. The simple lyric rides the smooth melody in a way that allows an important moment to play out over it. Norman asks Esther to marry him; her hesitation surfaces as she lightly improvises, just for their private moment, a little phrase to the tune in the background: "You drink too much," and then, "Yes." The romance is official when the playback reveals their conversation to all the musicians and crewmembers in the studio.

"It's a New World" is a sweetly direct declaration of love, sung along with the radio to begin, then segueing to a cappella, the orchestra sneaking back in midway. The rendition takes place in a small honeymoon hideaway and is performed just for Norman. The lyric, "though we're in a tiny room…" maybe hits the mark too closely, but in the first verse we hear the hint of "Over the Rainbow": "How wonderful that I'm beholding/A never-never land unfolding/Where we polish up the stars." (This song is my favorite from the film, although my mother favored "The Man That Got Away.") The scene is lovely—the momentary calm before the storm.

For Norman's personal entertainment at home, Esther, all second-wind energized after a long day at the studio, reenacts to the practice record the huge production number from her next film. Merging her speaking voice with her singing, a skill at which she was unmatched—Frank Sinatra being the only exception—Esther takes Norman through a full-scale performance. Explaining that the camera will pan in for a "big, fat close-up," Mama as Esther pulls her hands in to frame her face, her fingers splayed, and smiles—an iconic image that has been used to promote *A Star Is Born* on the original 1954 movie poster and in print advertisements, reissue posters, and home video artwork. After her close-up, Esther zips around the world: to Paris, to China, to Africa, to Brazil, in search of "Someone at Last." With a wide variety of Arlen rhythms and a minimum of Gershwin rhyme, Mama/Esther/Vicki is a force of nature, giving Norman his "surge of pleasure" after a humbling day as Mr. Lester. The film's last song, "Lose That Long Face," is placed

OPPOSITE: The most iconic image from *A Star Is Born* is this famous scene still of Vicki Lester describing her "big, fat close-up."

to contrast Esther's breakdown in her dressing room to the cheer-up number she is shooting on the soundstage. In despair over Norman's decline, Esther lays her soul bare for Oliver Niles. The scene is a masterpiece of writing and performance. Vicki confesses:

> You don't know what it's like to watch somebody you love just crumble away, bit by bit, day by day, in front of your eyes and stand there helpless. Love isn't enough. I thought it was. I thought I was the answer for Norman. But love isn't enough for him, and I'm afraid of what's beginning to happen. Within me. Because sometimes I hate him. I hate his promises to stop, and then the watching and waiting to see it begin again. I hate to go home to him at night and listen to his lies. Well, my heart goes out to him because he tries. He does try. But I hate him for failing. I hate me too. I hate me because I failed too. I have. I don't know what's going to happen to us, Oliver. No matter how much you love somebody, how do you live out the days? How?

Moss Hart understood when he wrote the sequence that Mama was both Norman Maine and Vicki Lester, that she would be speaking of her own failures and drug dependency. Cukor allowed Judy Garland the performer to be fully herself, thus creating such a moment of intensity and raw emotion that it is heartbreaking to watch. This release of unfiltered pain, probably more than any other scene in the film, confirmed Mama's gifts as not only as a singer and dancer, but as one of the great dramatic talents of her time as well.

OPPOSITE: Three images depicting the harrowing scene in which Vicki Lester shares her fears with Oliver Niles about Norman's addiction. Garland was describing her own problems. Mama was making a movie about addiction, but the characters were reversed. Cukor was quite the taskmaster on the set and there were many takes. Makeup artist Del Armstrong remembers driving Mama home at 9:00 p.m. after filming had completed. At one point, Mama was so overcome that Armstrong had to pull over and Mama threw up. Armstrong recalled, "It was just emotions—it wasn't from drinking—it was just an upheaval, a nervous disorder, like ulcers or something. I don't think she came to work the next day, either."

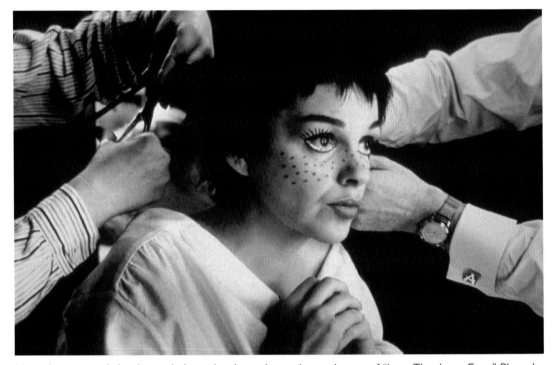

Mama being attended to by wardrobe and makeup during the production of "Lose That Long Face." Photo by Sanford Roth.

To contrast this moment, and to display her supremacy as a performer, as Vicki Lester she then shuffles to her mark to conclude the take. "Action!" is called; grinning Vicki the professional emerges to finish the shot. The tune is bouncy, suited for a tap dance, and Gershwin's words are amusing, the rhyming deliberately odd: "glum/vacu-um, panacea/idea, Peter Pan/sweeter pan, can see vacancy." (A discarded verse includes the oddity "critical/Pollyanna-lytical.") The whole of it is intended silliness that promotes the smilin' through, show-must-go-on inevitability that must be faced, no matter what. Esther needs to "turn that frown upside down." (How often did my mother do that? How many times did she fail?)

As musical director and conductor, Ray Heindorf was responsible for all the incidental and background music. However, the unsung hero was Skip Martin, the sole arranger and orchestrator credited on the film. He took the Arlen tunes, masterfully adapting them to situation

Mama's fatigue as both star and producer is shown in this image of her asleep on the set during production. Photo by Sanford Roth.

and character without intrusive bombast or complication. Relying on Heindorf to be his ears, George Cukor pulled off the incredible feat of helming his first movie musical after nearly twenty-five years of directing films.

Addended to the contract signed by Transcona Enterprises and Warner Bros. was a tentative list of directors acceptable to both parties: John Ford, Daniel Mann, Henry Koster, Charles Vidor, Michael Curtiz, and George Cukor. However, Mama was determined to secure Cukor. He had gained considerable status as a great director of actresses: Greta Garbo in *Camille* (1936), *A Woman's Face* (1941) starring Joan Crawford, *Gaslight* (1944) starring Ingrid Bergman, *Born Yesterday* (1950) with Judy Holliday, and a collaboration with Katharine Hepburn, whom he directed in ten films from 1932 to 1979, including *A Bill of Divorcement* (1932) and *The Philadelphia Story* (1940). In addition, there was Vivien Leigh, whom he guided in *Gone With the*

Wind (1939) until replaced by director Victor Fleming when producer David O. Selznick determined that Cukor wasn't making the film quickly enough. (Clark Gable, who feared the director was handing the epic to Leigh and turning it into a women's picture, was delighted that his old friend Fleming took over.) He had also directed *What Price Hollywood?* After turning down *A Star Is Born* (1937) (not wanting to dip too soon back in the same well), his interest was piqued by the idea of transforming not only the material, but Judy Garland, in high-production-value style.

Years earlier, Cukor had even been responsible for reining in the MGM artisans during preproduction of *The Wizard of Oz*, which Mama reported in a magazine interview. Her retelling sounds eerily similar to the process inflicted upon Esther Blodgett as a new starlet. "They tried to convert me into another person," she said. "They put a blonde wig on me and tried to change my nose, because it dipped too much, and they put caps all over my teeth. I looked like a male Mary Pickford by the time they got through with all the alterations."[7] My mother had remained grateful for Cukor's good taste and good sense; he was largely responsible for the final Dorothy look and performance, even though he did not direct the picture. As for Cukor, Judy Garland was someone he had wanted to direct ever since she attended a seventieth birthday party for Ethel Barrymore at his home. Garland sang an a cappella "Happy Birthday" that moved him and everyone at the party to tears.

The final bound script for *A Star Is Born*, Cukor's thirty-seventh film, dated October 7, 1953, ran 110 pages and totaled 119 scenes, excluding the lyrics to the musical numbers. The director was under contract to Loew's Incorporated (the parent company of MGM). Leow's had loaned him to Warner Bros. at a cost of $6,250 per week (Cukor received $4,000 per week for his services, the rest being pocketed by Loew's) with a twenty-week guarantee. With his team of designers and technicians, Cukor began work not only on his first musical, but his first color film and his first in widescreen. He familiarized himself with all three matters at once by testing CinemaScope and Technicolor versus WarnerColor during the

OPPOSITE, FROM TOP: George Cukor's expressive hands and intense style are demonstrated in this artistic image of Cukor directing Mama during production. • Cinematographer Sam Leavitt (left), Mama, and director George Cukor during production.

challenging number "The Man That Got Away." The scene was shot in multiple takes over several days in three iterations with many adjustments to the set and lighting, and to Mama's simple costume, as well. She not only lip-synced to her own recording, but my mother also sang along with it, full-out for every take, while never moving or gesturing the same way twice. She was reacting naturally to the mood of the music, allowing the story of the song to guide her vocal and physical performance.

> Cukor, an actress's best friend, firmly guided Mama through the rigors of Esther's emotional breakdown near the end of the picture.

For the opening sequence, Cukor made effective, even startling use of the wide screen: the limo-to-limo traffic, the sweep and buzz of the klieg lights, the snap, click, and flash of the press cameras, seen from above and in the glare of headlights. Up close, there are the arrivals of the celebrities to "Night of the Stars." It's 1954, but the vibe is very modern, the quick-cutting lending an urgency that energizes this updated Hollywood fable. Cukor handles the showbiz backstage with the jerk and surprise associated with a handheld camera. The chaos is organized, until Norman Maine shows up, drunk and ready to take on all comers: cowboys and horses, buskers and ballerinas. It is alarming to witness but fascinating to experience as Cukor's cameraman grabs it all with his very responsive lens, cutting between the pros onstage and the bedlam in the wings.

Cukor, an actress's best friend, firmly guided Mama through the rigors of Esther's emotional breakdown near the end of the picture. Her trust in him paid off. As production designer Gene Allen recalled, "The breakdown scene held a special interest for George from the very start. There were many takes for that scene....It fascinated him because it was so close to the real Judy Garland."[8]

OPPOSITE: Mama in conference with Cukor during production. Photo by Bob Willoughby.

James Mason, my mother, my father, George Cukor, and production designer Gene Allen on location during production.

Mama was physically ill before and during much of the filming of *A Star Is Born*. In addition to her constant struggles with her prescription medication and her fluctuating weight, my mother suffered from a severe premenstrual syndrome during this time, and endured a painful impacted wisdom tooth. Though she had Dr. Fred Pobirs to oversee her medication and Margaret Gundy as nurse and companion on the set to look after her, Mama was far from their ideal patient. She smoked Spud menthol cigarettes and sipped on vodka mixed with grape juice or Canadian Club whiskey with ginger ale throughout the production to settle her nerves. The pressures of the production were enormous for her.

Taskmaster George Cukor didn't coddle his star; he asked for take after take, pressing her further into her own emotional troubles to ground her performance—a Method acting approach before the Method was popular. Some takes left Mama sobbing uncontrollably. Cukor wrote to his friend, Katharine Hepburn, expressing his dismay in February

1954 as production was nearing its end. "About three weeks ago, strange, sinister and sad things began happening to Judy." She was always late, on the verge of derailing her own comeback. "This is the behavior of someone unhinged, but there is an arrogance and a ruthless selfishness that eventually alienates one's sympathy," Cukor wrote.[9] Both star and director were well aware that Judy/Esther was also Judy/Norman, one dynamic feeding and bleeding into the other. This duality informs the entire second half of the film. Mama identified with both main characters—a great, promising young talent brought low by addiction, self-loathing, and self-destruction.

In spite of what she may have put Cukor through—manic highs, incapacitating lows—his admiration for her rare gifts and his trust in her extraordinary instincts never wavered. He maintained that her qualities of warmth and vulnerability reminded him of the legendary Laurette Taylor, who gave one of the most lavishly praised performances of the twentieth century in Tennessee Williams's original Broadway production of *The Glass Menagerie* in 1945–1946.[10] Placing Mama on that same pedestal was an ultimate professional compliment. Furthermore, my mother had seen Taylor in *The Glass Menagerie* and met the great actress backstage after the performance. In spite of her reign of terror, what ended up on the screen demonstrated a new maturity in my mother's work, a breakout performance. *A Star Is Born* was intended—along with her new husband and me—a turning point to a new career for Judy Garland. My mother told journalist Bob Thomas in November 1953:

> I know it sounds awful to say, but I never really liked myself on the screen before. But now I go to the rushes and I actually enjoy them. I even cry a little at the sad scenes. The four years have done me a lot of good. I got out and met the people and sang before live audiences. It improved my timing, and my voice is better, too. I think I look better. I don't have that "little girl" look anymore.[11]

James Mason, Mama, and George Cukor enjoy a laugh during production.

From the outset, my parents really wanted Cary Grant as Norman Maine. They wined and dined him: lunches, dinners, golf games, and days at the racetrack. They did everything they could to talk him into doing this. The be-all, end-all matinee idol was intrigued, even spending time with Cukor rehearsing the part, but then demurred. Although Cukor had elevated Grant with such films as *Sylvia Scarlett* (1935), *Holiday* (1938), and *The Philadelphia Story* (1940), he was uncertain. The idea of unflattering self-commentary and the issue of alcoholism were obstacles he couldn't or wouldn't overcome. Mama herself was a factor in his decision: the trouble at MGM, the firing, and the attempted suicide had all been well documented. Grant appreciated her talent, but couldn't handle the baggage that came with it. His fee of $300,000

FROM LEFT: A portrait of a dashing Norman Maine as portrayed by James Mason. • A portrait of a drunken Norman Maine. OPPOSITE: Norman Maine and Vicki Lester attend the preview of her first starring film.

against 10 percent of the gross profits was also a deterrent. My parents were disappointed, and Mama, in retelling the story years later, remarked with her famous sense of humor, "God, I wish I could get back some of those dinners!" After Grant, the short list for one of the male roles of the year was odd in its diversity of age, experience, and temperament. The other approved actors were Laurence Olivier, Richard Burton, Tyrone Power, James Stewart, Gregory Peck, Ray Milland, Stewart Granger, Robert Taylor, and Glenn Ford. Two of my parents' friends were considered, but rejected by Warner: Humphrey Bogart was judged too old and Frank Sinatra was, incredibly, not considered a bankable talent in the early 1950s. Warner was keen to get Marlon Brando for the role, but he too declined.

Finally, a dark horse raced to the head of the pack. British export James Mason, in the end, was deemed the best choice for the charming scoundrel Maine. Mason, unlike Cary Grant,

leaped at the chance to work with Mama and to be directed by Cukor. Mason, a great English actor of British and American films, came into prominence with Carol Reed's *Odd Man Out* (1947) in his native England and starred as Brutus with Marlon Brando as Mark Antony in Joseph L. Mankiewicz's acclaimed film version of *Julius Caesar* (1953) for MGM. Mama was acquainted with Mason since he had worked with Vincente Minnelli in *Madame Bovary* (1949). Although Cukor was generally known as a "woman's director" (a label he resented), most savvy actors understood that Cukor was able to guide such leads as James Stewart (*The Philadelphia Story*), Ronald Colman (*A Double Life*), and later Rex Harrison (*My Fair Lady*) to Best Actor Oscar wins. Mason's best-remembered films include Stanley Kubrick's *Lolita* (1962), Alfred Hitchcock's *North by Northwest* (1959), and Sidney Lumet's *The Verdict* (1982). As for Mama, Mason recalled her as a delightful human being, "Judy was essentially a witty, lively, talented, funny, adorable woman.... Over

Norman Maine slaps his wife during her moment onstage to receive her Academy Award.

113

and above her musical talent she was as funny as Lucille Ball, another lady of genius, and could have been as heartbreaking as Chaplin at his very best."[12] Despite his costar's unreliable work habits, James Mason held fond memories of my mother and his experience on *A Star Is Born*. He remembered in his autobiography:

> Judy was not always reliable, in fact there were some days when she would not really be fighting fit until after the lunch break . . . . If the film went over budget only a very small fraction of the overage was due to Judy's erratic time table. . . . Judy was by no means a temperamental star. "Temperamental star" is usually a euphemism for selfish and bad tempered, and a temperamental star of this sort can be a *real* time-waster. I have worked with some. And they are more rampant now than they used to be. But this was not Judy.[13]

The Moss Hart/James Mason incarnation of Maine is a far more predatory and volatile creation than the Fredric March character from 1937. Mason is hair-trigger, ready to rumble, but with a generous, nurturing inner nature to call upon. Out of Esther's lovely raw material he forms Vicki Lester, just as Pygmalion sculpted Galatea and Professor Higgins shaped Eliza Doolittle. Naturally, he falls in love with his creation.

"Mr. Maine's charm escapes me. It always has," Matt Libby says wearily. Public relations man Libby has a tense, serial battle going with Maine, who creates chaos that Libby must de-escalate. Jack Carson does expert work inhabiting workaholic Libby; he is street-smart, a tough talker, and brings to the role a physicality that Lionel Stander lacked. Carson was a popular, wise-cracking character actor, best remembered for playing Wally Fay in *Mildred Pierce* starring Joan Crawford, and as "Gooper" in the film version of *Cat on a Hot Tin Roof* (1958). A core player on the Warner Bros. lot, Carson had been friends with my mother for years; in fact, they knew each other back in Mama's vaudeville days. Against Mason's brittle star power, Carson makes the two an even match.

Matt Libby (Jack Carson) confronts Norman Maine (James Mason) at the racetrack.

To studio chief Oliver Niles, Charles Bickford brought the experience of nearly seventy-five motion pictures, such as *Anna Christie* (1930), *Of Mice and Men* (1939), and *Johnny Belinda* (1948), and had earned three Academy Award nominations for supporting roles as well as the respect of his peers. Not the natty, worldly Adolphe Menjou, Bickford portrays a benevolent, open-minded, yet straight-talking movie mogul with a powerful, gruff speaking voice. He is loyal to Maine, fatherly to Esther, and a close relative to actor Millard Mitchell's performance as R. F. Simpson, the sympathetic big boss he portrayed in *Singin' in the Rain* (1952). Actual studio chiefs were hardly this benign. (William Powell was offered the part, but was not inclined to relegate himself to below-the-title roles.)

Danny McGuire was developed out of the sketch that was Grandma Lettie, mixed with a trace of Andy Devine from 1937, to create Esther's accompanist, then vocal arranger, and, it seems, her only friend. Young character actor Tom Noonan had to wait for the picture's end to grab a moment in the spotlight. Noonan was best known at the time of production for his supporting role as Gus Esmond, fiancé of Marilyn Monroe's character in *Gentlemen Prefer Blondes* (1953). According to Cukor, Noonan rose to the task as Danny shocks Esther out of her self-pity. Cukor recalled of the filming of one of the film's big emotional scenes:

The press photographs Norman Maine (protected by Vicki and Oliver Niles) after Norman has been released from jail.

Toward the end of shooting we had to do a scene when she's in a state of total depression after her husband's suicide. While we lined it up she just sat there, very preoccupied. . . . Just before the take I said to her very quietly, "You know what this is about. You really know this." She gave me a look, and I knew she was thinking, "He wants me to dig into myself because I know all about this in my own life." That was all. We did a take. . . . a friend, played by Tommy Noonan, comes to see her to try and persuade her to go to a benefit performance that night. He chides her about not giving in to herself, he even gets deliberately rough with her—and she loses her head. She gets up and screams like someone out of control, maniacal and terrifying. And when Judy Garland did this, it was *absolutely* terrifying! She had no concern with what she looked like, she went much further than I'd expected, and I thought it was great. . . . So he grabbed her and held her and spoke his next lines with great force and energy. The lines were meant to shame her—and her reaction was unforgettable. She turned around, and you saw that all the anger and madness and fear had disappeared. Her face looked very vulnerable and tender, there were tears in her eyes. So I said, "Cut!" and then, "Quick let's do it once more!". . . . So Judy did it again—differently but just as stunningly. . . . Anyway, when it was over, I said to Judy, "You really scared the hell out of me." She was very pleased, she didn't realize what an effect she'd made. And then—she was always funny, she had this great humor—she said, "Oh, that's nothing. Come over to my house any afternoon. I do it every afternoon." Then she gave me a look and added, "But I only do it *once* at home."[14]

Being a baby at the time, I, of course, don't recall those days. But in the years to come, our home would be transformed into a battleground, noisy and combative, as my father became less and less my mother's champion. Dad started out crazy about Mama and ended up being driven just plain crazy. As the variety of chemicals in my mother's system caused her moods to swing up and down, she would pick fights with my dad seemingly out of the blue. But their volatile arguments started later. During the filming of *A Star Is Born*, I envision them as a mutually supportive team. Dad, like James Mason and others on the set, felt protective of my mercurial mama.

One memory of my mother comes from Lucy Marlow, an actress with a small featured role in the film as a movie starlet. On Oliver Niles's arm at the "Night of the Stars," she preens as Lola Lavery for the newsreel cameras in her black sheath and soufflé of white fox fur, diamonds nestled in her sleek up-done hair. They pause for the radio interviewer (Joan Shawlee, later to be Sweet Sue, leader of the all-girl band in Billy Wilder's 1959 classic *Some Like It Hot*), who gushes, "Did you ever see anyone so sweet, so unspoiled, and down-to-earth? She's a darling girl." Marlow, who had been cautioned to tread lightly around the star on set, found herself struggling to unfasten her very tight bodice. Mama stepped in to help and confided, "Listen honey, I've got my money in this thing. If George says you're doing something to help the picture, I'm all for you—you're all right in my book."[15] That is the warm and welcoming side of my mother, though she was just as capable of an abrupt about-face, raging and shoveling up a mountain out of a slight molehill. George Cukor, the hands-on expert on the star for the duration of the shoot, had his patience and professional demeanor put to the test frequently by her unstable muddle of ego and insecurity. But he always countered his frank assessments with assurances that "Judy Garland was a very original and resourceful actress."[16] There was no prototype for Judy Garland except Judy Garland herself.

Cukor's movies often display an expressive use of composition within the frame. He knew not only how to shape a performance, but how to place it within the entire structure of a movie. The character, the colors, the position within the composition, were to be of utmost importance to him for this film. However, this was Cukor's first color film. To offset his inexperience with Technicolor, he enlisted his friend, the renowned Russian-born fashion photographer George Hoyningen-Huene, as color consultant and to create the overall color design

OPPOSITE: Jack Carson, Mama, and James Mason. Mama made a point to be available on the set for her fellow actors. However, when she was not needed, she enjoyed Bette Davis's old dressing room on the Warner Bros. studio lot in Burbank.

for the film. Hoyningen-Huene's experience with *Harper's Bazaar* and in documentary film-making resulted in his use of dark, muted hues as a conduit of emotion and meaning. Later, the photographer expressed his view that "Color pictures usually have too much color. Color should be disciplined and an emotional stimulant."[17] The restrained color chart for "The Man That Got Away," in its final form, is rich yet subtle in its mix of a nostalgic shade of rose red and mahogany backing up the navy blue of my mother's simple dress.

The "art boys," as Cukor called them, were led by Gene Allen in his return to the Warner design department. Allen began on the production as a sketch artist, but quickly oversaw all the scenic renderings and storyboarding, which included composition, lighting, and costumes, in his multiple duties. It ultimately led to his being credited as the film's production designer and commenced a long professional collaboration with Cukor. Allen's assistant, Malcolm Bert, assumed the position of art director, working closely with Hoyningen-Huene. The collaboration between all of these great talents is truly remarkable, and I find something to marvel at with every viewing. For example, the 2.35:1 aspect ratio matte paintings to simulate exterior backgrounds (in the days before digital technology) are theatrical but add a great deal to the production value of the film.

The esteemed cinematographer Harry Stradling, who photographed Garland's *Easter Parade*, *The Pirate*, and *In the Good Old Summertime*, was to be cinematographer, but the delays in pre-production forced him to leave to fulfill a prior commitment. Sam Leavitt, Stradling's frequent camera operator, came on board as his replacement. Leavitt began as an assistant camera operator in the 1930s, working his way up the ladder. His best-known credits, in addition to *A Star Is Born*, include the Otto Preminger films *Carmen Jones* (1954) and *Exodus* (1960) as well as Stanley Kramer's *The Defiant Ones* (1958), for which he won an Academy Award for his cinematography.

Part of Cukor's research during the preproduction phase was viewing *The Robe*, the landmark production in color and widescreen. He was a quick study, just like his star. Just as

OPPOSITE: Mama sharing a laugh with assistant dance director Jack Harmon (left) and designer Irene Sharaff (right) during production of the "Born in a Trunk" sequence.

he had been an early pioneer during the transition period of silent films to "talkies," Cukor assessed the new, primitive technology as he faced the challenge of telling an intimate story in the colossal dimensions of CinemaScope. He dismissed the so-called "rules" and insisted his team find solutions. He strove for atmosphere, detail, low-key lighting, depth of field, and color shading and texture in every single frame.

The visual quality resulting from the work of Cukor and his colleagues is stunning, a step ahead of the work being done elsewhere. The Cocoanut Grove—when Maine is on the prowl—is a shadowed harem of 2:00 a.m. stale smoke air, as Maine moves among the towering palms, as if stalking his prey in the jungle. The Downbeat Club, nearly closed for the night, is dim and blasé, a den of cast-off jazz, and a bold choice for a Technicolor musical. Test footage shows the club from setup to setup, descending into darkness, as Cukor and his team focus less

Mama in an early conception of her chanteuse costume in "The Peanut Vendor" flashback from the "Born in a Trunk" sequence. Designer Irene Sharaff replaced the costume for the more flattering dress seen in the final version of the film.

FROM LEFT: Mama rests on a dressing table and consults with an unidentified man during a break in production. • A portrait of Mama singing "My Melancholy Baby" from the "Born in a Trunk" sequence. This portrait was later used as the cover of *Judy*, Mama's 1956 studio album for Capitol Records. Photo by Bob Willoughby.

light on the proceedings. The bar is behind a scrim (a theatrical term for a gauze cloth screen or backdrop), and thus rendered an abstraction—just a backdrop for the bravura performance. A scrim is employed again at the preview card reading scene and later at the party at the beach house. In one memorable moment, Norman and Esther embrace in semi-close-up, while guests barely move behind the scrim. They are almost mannequins, lit in rose tones, elegant, and spruce. An expansive aviary displays large, exotic, plumed white birds perched on the branches of a flowering tree. It's a fitting setting for Norman's moment with just-born star Esther on the terrace: the fame and the glamour of Hollywood are symbolized in the mansion aglow behind them and the city glittering below. As Norman reminds Esther, it's all hers for the taking.

The Maines' brightly lit midcentury modern (as it would be referred to today) beach house in Malibu is where Esther stages her global trip around the living room for Norman. She employs practically every stick of furniture and bit of decor to entertain her out-of-work husband. It is an ingenious swap for a huge, expensive production number, designed and dressed to the hilt. (The house on Mapleton Drive, where we lived until the autumn of 1960, would see these treasures installed as soon as production wrapped.) Near the end, the beach house is dimmed for Maine's last scenes. He pauses at the back door for one more look, then heads for the shore. Cukor stages the final swim much as Wellman did in 1937, but with the improvement of a deluxe panoramic Pacific Ocean view. A beach in Laguna, California, stood in for Malibu's private coast. A few well-chosen locations lend the movie the grit and authenticity it might have lacked without them. The Shrine is a big hanger of an auditorium, but its daunting size ramps up the sense of possibility. Stan's Drive-In in Hollywood, long-gone, is where Esther serves up nut-burgers. Piru, California, at that time a wide dirt road in search of a town, is the elopement destination. The Cocoanut Grove, the Lincoln Heights Jail, the Santa Anita Racetrack, and the Lancaster Hotel on Bunker Hill in downtown Los Angeles portray themselves, as does the Church of the Good Shepherd in Beverly Hills, its front steps the platform for a mob of fans, press, and police.

Working closely with Gene Allen was costume designer Mary Ann Nyberg, Her résumé included *Lili* (1953) and *The Band Wagon* (1953), both receiving some attention. The dresses, gowns, dance costumes, and sportswear Nyberg created for Cyd Charisse in the latter film must have convinced my parents that she had the talent to work a little magic. (At age thirty-one, Mama's life of nonstop work had caught up with her, making her look a few years older.) The costume budget with thirty changes for the star nearly doubled to $100,000, due to several contingencies: Mama's weight gains and losses, her changes of mood and mind, her borrowing of the wardrobe for personal use and returning it in sorry shape, and her trickery in rejecting a new piece, only to pack it up and take home! Also, the script was in a constant state of reconsideration, wreaking havoc on both preproduction and production. Nyberg's initial excitement to

OPPOSITE: Mama and James Mason during production of the Academy Awards sequence.

ABOVE: Vicki Lester receives her Academy Award. OPPOSITE: Filming Vicki Lester receiving her Academy Award. One of the incongruities of the film is having the Academy Awards depicted as a banquet held at the Cocoanut Grove. Although that is how Mama remembered the Academy Awards in her early years (she received her juvenile award at the Cocoanut Grove in 1940), by the 1950s the Academy Awards ceremony ceased to be an intimate banquet and had evolved into an event held in a large theater such as Grauman's Chinese or the RKO Pantages in Hollywood.

be working on Mama's big star vehicle turned to dread. My mother had a problematic figure to clothe. At four-foot-eleven and one hundred pounds at her ideal weight, she was certainly petite, but when carrying extra weight, she appeared not to have a defined waistline, her hips seeming to emerge directly from her small chest. Her long, slim legs were her pride and joy, and those must be given room to shine. She was a costume designer's challenge.

More than halfway through the picture, Nyberg stormed off the production, unhappy with her treatment and her nerves frayed by the demands of the production. Nevertheless, most of Mama's wardrobe was designed by Nyberg, with the balance by Jean Louis and Irene Sharaff. Some observers credit Nyberg, some Jean Louis, for the Vicki Lester Academy Awards gown, which replaced an initial white design. The dramatic dress we see is midnight blue with long sleeves and a stand-up collar. It has a sculpted train heavily beaded in a peacock feather motif. This gown denotes the emergence of a more sophisticated woman, a full-blown celebrity ready to embrace her fame and reap the rewards. But this dual-duty dress is also the gown associated with the humiliation of Esther, as Maine hijacks her big moment. The clothing for Norman Maine is not specifically credited, but was selected carefully and fit superbly, as a matinee idol's would be. James Mason being a gentleman actor, his Fred Astairian wardrobe of suits and tuxedos is understated and elegant, as are the casual tweed jacket, polo-neck sweater, and charcoal trousers worn when Norman de-glams Esther. At film's end, Maine is de-glamorized himself, humbled to a plain white terry-cloth robe, shortly to be shed, sullied in wet sand, and then washed away in the tide. Along with James Mason's costumes came a new wardrobe for my father. Dad, early on in preproduction, had suits custom-tailored for himself at a cost of $75,000. He charged the expense to the movie's budget, but not without Jack Warner getting wind of it. Warner realized he would have to keep a closer eye on expense sheets and branded my father an opportunist.

Filming the Academy Awards scene in which Vicki Lester wins her Oscar for *A World for Two*. Cinematographer Sam Leavitt (wearing hat) is behind the camera.

Preproduction absorbed much of 1953. The spring and summer were expended with pre-production duties. As for my father, it was all-consuming to hold my mother together while producing such an elaborate, prestige picture with little experience to his credit beyond two Monogram "B" pictures of no consequence.

In late August 1953, Mama officially began work on *A Star Is Born* at Warner Bros. studios in Burbank. The mood was upbeat, though a cloud of doubt and resentment still hung over her alma mater in Culver City. Down on the MGM lot, Arthur Freed, slighted for not having been consulted on the ambitious undertaking by his former wunderkind, grumbled about my parents' project, "Those two alley cats can't make a picture."[18] But make a picture they did, beginning with a flurry of dance rehearsals, sessions for prerecording of Mama's songs, wardrobe fittings and tests, and makeup and hair trials. Vern Alves, a friend of my father's, was hired as the film's associate producer. He served as gofer to both my parents and helped keep things moving. Second-unit location shooting at various sites was under way.

The first day of filming at Warner Bros. was Monday, October 12, 1953. My father gave my mother a bracelet that day engraved, "Columbus discovered America on October 12, 1492. Judy Garland began principal photography on *A Star Is Born* on October 12, 1953. With all my love—Sid." The inaugural scene before the cameras was Esther as an extra, her face unseen as she waves the scarf from the train window. Technical issues forced five takes of the brief scene, covering one-and-a-half script pages and costing $25,000. Shooting continued on the lot and on location through mid-April 1954. Warner studio logs indicate that Mama was often absent or left work early. Illness and fatigue were blamed.

Initially budgeted at $3 million, the final cost was twice that figure, making *A Star Is Born* the most expensive movie ever shot in Hollywood at that time. Unfortunately, the industry blamed my mother almost entirely. I believe this was unfair. Taking into account her whims and eccentricities, the truth remains that Mama, when on her game, was a prepared professional. She was also lightning fast—one rehearsal and she was ready to roll; one reading of a page and her lines were committed to memory. Her photographic memory was extraordinary.

In fact, having a mother with such perfect recall was terrifying when I lied to her on occasion as a young teenager! She possessed a brilliant mind and was a voracious reader. She was a uniquely gifted singer at the height of her vocal prowess, a supple comedienne, and a naturally instinctive actress who withheld nothing. Ina Claire, the actress and friend of Cukor's, visited the set and observed a difficult, emotion-filled scene. On the set, Cukor was tough with her, but never an instance of directorial overreach. Later, still amazed, she told him, "That girl should work two hours, and then be taken home in an ambulance! How she gives of herself!"[19]

Initially budgeted at $3 million, the final cost was twice that figure, making *A Star Is Born* the most expensive movie ever shot in Hollywood at that time.

Other celebrities stopped by the Warner lot to have a look and congratulate Mama on her return. Louella O. Parsons kept the newspapers buzzing about her comeback, filling many column inches with report and speculation, some negative, some positive. Hedda Hopper did the same, although she was not invited to the studio as Parsons was, because my mother loathed Hopper. But old and new friends with no agenda also dropped in, like Elizabeth Taylor, Guy Madison, Ginger Rogers, Mervyn LeRoy, Clifton Webb, Sarah Churchill, Teresa Wright, and Jean Simmons. Mama also welcomed Doris Day and Leslie Caron, all three ladies perhaps exchanging "war stories" about working in the trenches of the Hollywood musical comedy factory. Kay Thompson, my mother's mentor and vocal coach in the Arthur Freed unit at MGM, visited the set and offered moral support. There is something about the first number, "Gotta Have Me Go With You," and its lady/chorus boy patter and step that recalls Kay's famous nightclub act, "Kay Thompson and the Williams Brothers," including Andy, the youngest, that toured the country in the late 1940s and early 1950s. Kay may have offered some input to Mama and her choreographer, Richard Barstow. Kay was always around, as

my mother's close friend and Liza's god-mother. She is perhaps best remembered as the author of the Eloise series of children's books (the first was published in 1955). We stayed close for the next forty years.

Liza and myself—ages seven and one, respectively, during this period—did not have our mother at hand; we were cared for by nannies. Tucked away in the manicured, peaceful enclave of Holmby Hills, we were far from the soundstages of the movie business. But we did sometimes visit. I still have photographs of us with Mama on the set of *A Star Is Born*. She was shooting scenes and posing for pictures. She was being fitted for costumes. She was rehearsing dance steps and recording songs. She was doing publicity interviews. Amid the frenzied whirl of starring in her comeback film, she was trying to be a wife, and doing her best to be a loving mother. And all this was done under the influence, in a cloud or on a high. When she came home every evening, exhausted from the day, my mother somehow mustered the energy to give at least two more performances before bed—a lullaby for Liza, and one for me.

ABOVE: Mama with Liza and me during production of the "Born in a Trunk" sequence. Photo by Bob Willoughby. OPPOSITE: Leslie Caron (center) and Elizabeth Taylor (right) visit Mama during production of the "Born in a Trunk" sequence.

133

Mama was an extrovert and enjoyed being social. If there was a dinner party, an opportunity to play cards, or sing around the piano, she would find the energy for that as well. Mama was part of the original "Rat Pack," a group of neighbors in Holmby Hills that included Frank Sinatra (pack master), Mama (first vice president), my father (cage master), Humphrey Bogart (rat in charge of public relations), Lauren Bacall (den mother), and Irving "Swifty" Lazar (treasurer). Mike and Gloria Romanoff and David and Hjördis Niven were also part of the pack. They were all night owls who lived close to one another, and loved to drink and laugh. If a light was on, any member might knock on the door for a game of cards, a nightcap, or conversation. Gossip columnist Sheilah Graham referred to the tight-knit Holmby Hills group as a "rat pack." Lazar thought the label hilarious, and encouraged the nickname by creating little stickpins, shaped like rats, with rubies for eyes and gave them to all the original members.

After wrapping principal photography, my parents both became convinced that the film lacked a crucial element. A substantial, even lengthy, production number needed to be inserted as part of the sneak preview of Vicki Lester's first motion picture. It should be a movie within the movie, a literal tale of a rising star, lavishly appointed, a number to top all numbers. (Maybe they had a point. *A Star Is Born* has no other monumental moment of song and dance.) Mama's ambition for her picture had been super-charged by the grand success of her ex-husband Vincente Minnelli's *An American in Paris* (1951) which, in its broad scope and arty pretensions, had been named Best Picture by the Academy at its 1952 ceremony, and was the first musical in quite some time to be so honored. The closing seventeen-minute ballet, built around George Gershwin's symphonic tone poem, almost seemed to be the reason the film was made in the first place. Every scene and song prepared the way for the big finish. For her movie, Mama wanted something comparable, preferably even to outshine it. Arlen and Gershwin had written three numbers to consider. The duo wrote "I'm Off the Downbeat," "Green Light Ahead," and "Dancing Partner" for the crucial sequence. All three disappointed Mama and underwhelmed Dad. The two agreed they wanted something more grandly scaled, something that boldly declared in words and music, "I'm back!"

The idea had the sharp pull of a challenge. My ambitious mother turned to her "source," the Freed unit music men, primarily Roger Edens, her mentor and friend from her earliest days at MGM, and his right-hand collaborator Leonard Gershe. Edens was under contract at Metro, so he agreed to a hush-hush arrangement; Gershe would work on a freelance basis. Mama was thinking of the autobiographical opener that Edens had conceived for her engagement at the Palace in New York in 1951 and 1952. Edens proposed that the number "Born in a Trunk" be expanded from that basic opener idea from the Palace to become a framework for an autobiographical musical showstopper: art imitating life as a woman sings her trajectory from vaudeville obscurity to Broadway star. Edens and Mama auditioned the new concept, with Dad as cheerleader, for Jack Warner, who, in a surprising display of full support, approved an additional $250,000 to design, rehearse, and shoot it. The schedule was very tight, as the film was locked into its late September premiere date. When Hedda Hopper got wind that a lavish new number was to be added to an already large-scale production, she couldn't resist a quip in her *Los Angeles Times* column. "When I asked why Warners would spend money on a ballet [sic] sequence in *Star* when the picture already cost $4,500,000 and runs three hours and twenty minutes," she wrote, "I was told that after that much, why quibble over another $200,000 to make it better?"[20]

As soon as Warner gave the green light, Leonard Gershe set about finishing the lyrics to "Born in a Trunk," which would be a stylized facsimile of Mama's own showbiz-in-the-blood career path. My mother's first professional billing was in December 1924. At the Grand Theatre, the three Gumm sisters entertained in songs and dances: Baby Frances, two years old, Virginia, seven, and Mary Jane, nine. Francis "Frank" Gumm co-owned the Grand, and was in charge of the box office. On June 10, 1922 (after reconsidering a planned abortion), he and his wife welcomed Frances Ethel Gumm, named for both of them. Ethel was accompanying her daughters on the piano, so it may have been Baby Frances's grandmother who pushed her out onstage the very first time to sing "Jingle Bells." She never needed another shove. In fact, according to legend, Frank had to go up onstage and carry her off. But my mother was a master of selectively recalling her past, reinventing the truth in story after story. Mama always did prefer her own versions of reality. How could she remember what happened that night? She was only two years old!

The Gumm Sisters became half-sized vaudevillians, traveling by train and playing the Northeast and the West. One trip took them to Southern California, where stage mother Ethel was taken with the mild weather. In 1927, the Gumms moved to Lancaster, California, in the Antelope Valley, seventy miles northeast of Los Angeles. Frank managed a movie theater, and Ethel kept her eyes and ears open for word of auditions in Hollywood. The Gumm Sisters performed onstage at the Shrine Auditorium, on the radio at KNX and KFWB, and in four short films in which Baby Gumm stole the show. Baby Gumm appeared as a solo act, on occasion, at the Cocoanut Grove's "Star Night" series (Mama's history with the nightclub going way back to 1932). The sisters continued to perform together, while Baby, the attention-getter, was catered to, indulged—maybe spoiled a bit. Frank and Ethel began a series of separations, his bisexuality one of their issues. Ethel moved the girls to an L.A. suburb, then to Silver Lake, on the eastern edge of Hollywood. Frank, in declining health, remained alone in Lancaster, joining his family only sporadically. At the Oriental Theatre in Chicago in 1934, vaudeville star George Jessel suggested that since Gumm rhymed with "glum," the Gumm Sisters should change their name. Jessel suggested "Garland" as a surname after the New York drama critic, Robert Garland. A variant version of this story is that Jessel thought they resembled a garland of flowers when they sang together. Another tale, told by my mother herself, refers to the 1928 song "Judy" with music by Hoagy Carmichael and a lyric by Sammy Lerner, which she loved. She maintained that if she was to change her last name, she could now change her first name as well and become "Judy." However it happened, Baby Frances Gumm became known as Judy Garland.

Helen Morgan's "Bill" (from the great 1927 Oscar Hammerstein II and Jerome Kern musical *Show Boat*) was just one of the mature-themed torch songs Mama sang in the act. When she let loose with her trumpery belt, she could be heard in the back of the balcony, without a microphone, at age twelve. The Garland Sisters, on Ethel's improvised tour, performed in Detroit, Milwaukee, Kansas City, Denver, all over Los Angeles, San Francisco, and at Lake Tahoe until August 1935. Frank, feeling more and more isolated in Lancaster, moved into the Silver Lake residence. Midsummer 1935 was a pivotal time. Ethel, through a chain of contacts, scheduled an audition for Mama at MGM with Louis B. Mayer, for whom she sang "Zing! Went the Strings of My Heart." After three auditions for MGM, a screen test was arranged, directed by musician Roger Edens. Mayer, encouraging but not enthusiastic, offered a studio contract at $100 per week. It was now October; my mother was just thirteen.

Within weeks, Frank Gumm passed away, victim to the spinal meningitis that had been present in his system for years. Mama later noted that her father made her feel emotionally safe and protected. Indeed, much of her makeup as a person came from her father. He was her champion, her safety net, and he made it clear that he didn't care if she chose to continue singing or not. He loved her unconditionally. It was her mother who kept pushing. When my grandfather died, when my mother was so young, her primary parental emotional support was taken away from her. In her mind, she lost the one person who was on her side. Proving herself at MGM and grieving for her father mingled prematurely and uneasily in the teenager's fragile psyche. Success in Hollywood would be used—precariously—as the basis for validation of her worth as a person.

Mama reminisced happily about her vaudeville years, a time she wanted to reference, as the pieces of "Born in a Trunk" were assembled.

A woman-child stepped through the mighty gates of MGM in late 1935. She had been working since age two, maturing professionally, but not personally. Her clarion voice, with all its color and brass, was her calling card, but a strong inner sense of identity had yet to be acquired, and she blamed her mother for that. From there, Metro-Goldwyn-Mayer, home of

Garbo and Gable and Harlow, took over. Ethel Gumm was left behind, in the stir of stardust, and in her daughter's selective memory. Mama reminisced happily about her vaudeville years, a time she wanted to reference, as the pieces of "Born in a Trunk" were assembled. She was part of a family of troupers, scraping for a living, split weeks from Poughkeepsie to Pocatello, Idaho, "dressing rooms and hotel rooms and waiting rooms and rooms behind-the-scenes." It was a hardscrabble life, but Mama did well with traveling, with suitcases, with strangers, and with uncertainty. She toddled onto the stage like a little pro, blessed with a big voice and a star presence to back it up. The audience was as eager to applaud her as she was to receive their applause.

Roger Edens and Leonard Gershe, my mother's two miracle men, shaped her personal past into "Born in a Trunk," an intimate panorama of song, dance, and comedy, an all-American pastiche of entertainment nostalgia. This was the moment for Vicki Lester to wow the sneak-previewers, and for Judy Garland to electrify the critics, the moviegoers, and maybe the Academy of Motion Picture Arts and Sciences, too. "Born in a Trunk" was crafted as the framing device to feature some classic American Songbook tunes: "I'll Get By," "You Took Advantage of Me," "Black Bottom," "The Peanut Vendor," "Melancholy Baby," and "Swanee." The goal was to capture the essence of MGM Freed Unit complexity—hokey, arty, and slangy all at once. *An American in Paris* was the impetus, but *Singin' in the Rain* (1952) and *The Band Wagon* (1953) were other inspiring benchmarks of craft and creativity, each offering an appealing and sexy song-and-dance sequence, a musical climax. "Born in a Trunk" has no sexual overtones, and the girl is neither Leslie Caron nor Cyd Charisse. But it does have Mama, the girl-next-door who can clown like Chaplin, and sing like…well, like no one else but Judy Garland.

The production team differed greatly from the movie itself. George Cukor had moved on to his next project. (He couldn't endorse the high-concept extravagance, anyway.) Dance director Richard Barstow and Roger Edens replaced him in the director's chair. Irene Sharaff served as art director, but Gene Allen took on the scene design, leaving the costumes to Sharaff. The new cinematographer was Harold Rosson (*The Wizard of Oz* and *Singin' in the Rain*) who

OPPOSITE: Dance director Richard Barstow and Mama rehearsing.

139

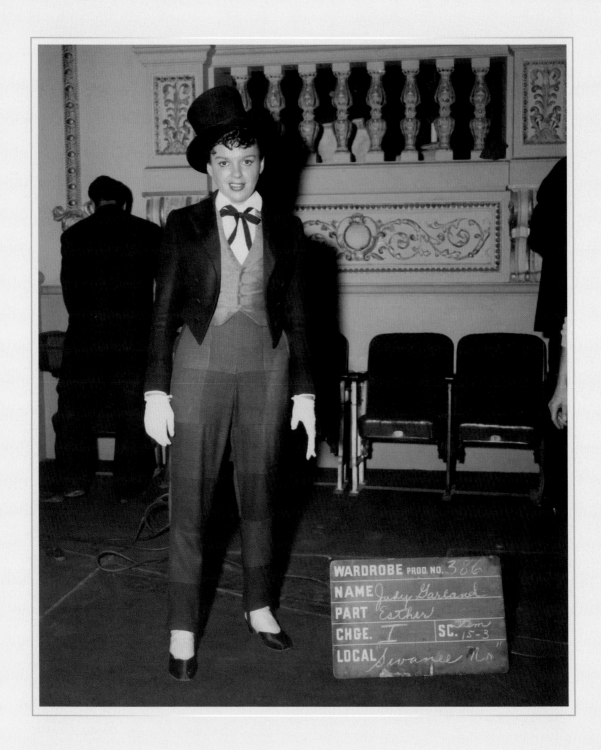

ABOVE: Mama, from the "Born in a Trunk" sequence. OPPOSITE: A wardrobe test photograph of Mama for the "Swanee" sequence in "Born in a Trunk."

already had a relationship with Mama and with Technicolor. Richard Barstow would continue as choreographer. My father came up with the very efficient plan to shoot at night, citing to Jack Warner the distinct advantages. It was summer, and the soundstages would easily rise above ninety degrees during the day; my mother could pre-record and have her costumes fitted at Western Costume during the day while the dancers rehearsed; and, Mama, being a self-confessed "nighthawk," would respond positively to the nocturnal schedule.

Night shooting began June 30, 1954, with "Swanee." The twelve-minute "Born in a Trunk" kicks off with that number, set before a depiction of the French Quarter in New Orleans, moving on to a modest vaudeville stage, then backstage. A satire of big-time corporate entertainment is next, in business gray, soulless and rat-racy. A bit of burlesque dances in with a chorus line; a seedy bar gives way to a club of little renown, which disappears to reveal a chic supper club, for a sophisticated rendition of "Melancholy Baby." Broadway calls next, the big finale returning, which opened the whole sequence. Mama is the girl singer at the center of this travelogue, progressing to her dream of the Great White Way, as a star. Along the way are parallels to her real-life journey: the family, the small child brought on to "milk the applause," the child, now a young girl, sent out to sing solo, then the death of a parent, here the mother (which was later cut from the sequence). The narrative takes its own course at this point, but the references are noteworthy. One last moment of Mama's art imitating life would be the famous Broadway producer who discovers the star-to-be, a stand-in for Louis B. Mayer.

Irene Sharaff cleverly used a single basic pattern for all of Mama's "Trunk" dresses, a tightly corseted sweetheart bodice with a drop-waist and crinoline full skirt. Depending on the scene, the dress has various sleeve lengths, and is collared uptight or strapless, again in a variety of blues. Sharaff succeeded

in giving the leading lady that which she was not naturally endowed with: an elegant long torso and a tiny waist. The last gown is a John Singer Sargent–like minor masterwork— Mama's opera-gloved arm and hand resting on the piano in a pose fit for a canvas—strapless but topped with an asymmetrical bolero, beautifully framing her neck and face. In the number that opens and closes the sequence, Mama is in a variation of one of her signature

A wide shot depicting the length of the CinemaScope image during production of "Swanee," the final song in the "Born in a Trunk" medley. The Al Jolson standard became closely identified with my mother's later concerts.

looks: a man's tailcoat and plaid trousers, with white gloves and spats, finished off with a top hat and cane. Her makeup is heavy and distinct for these scenes and for the "Black Bottom" number. Here, my mother's black eyeliner, faux lashes, and cropped dark wig presage my

143

sister Liza's look, fifteen years ahead. I still marvel at how fresh, natural, and young Mama appears in this showbiz pastiche.

For "Born in a Trunk," Gene Allen's scenic design is painterly, abstracted, suggestive rather than explicit. Every number is a mini-musical, each with its own esthetic. Allen's lines are soft—the warren of agency offices in high perspective the exception—the palette colorful but washed, the opening and closing explosion of red another exception. When the deep red curtain closes on our girl's Broadway debut, the setting becomes red on red as banks of roses and anemones, scarlet and vermillion, bloom in the background. In front of this floral expanse, she begins to sing her story. The supper club near the end is its opposite, grayed and blued, with monumental "frescos" peering over the singer forming the cumulative effect of an antique mural.

The inclusion of "Born in a Trunk" has its detractors. It has been derided as overproduced, a distraction, and out of key with the rest of the film. It has been criticized as unnecessary, since Esther's talent has already been established, memorably, with "The Man That Got Away." The counter opinion is that "Born in a Trunk" provides the ideal platform for Esther's comic skills and timing—as well as her vocal flexibility—to shine. At no other point in the film are Mama/Esther's wit, showmanship, and indomitable spirit allowed such free rein. She is able to enact her connections to, and affection for, the grand traditions of live American entertainment. At the time, the number may have smacked of self-indulgence. Today, this twelve-minute sample of the Garland touch is hailed as a classic high point in my mother's lengthy career. In the summer of 2017, "Born in a Trunk" was met with a thundering reception when screened at the Hollywood Bowl as part of a Los Angeles Philharmonic concert. But, George Cukor voiced the majority opinion, "It fits in quite well, but it seems to me to tell another story—or, at least, a story within a story. The main flow of the narrative was very powerful and well developed, and anything which interferes with that flow seems to me wrong."[21] The *A Star is Born* company wrapped for the second time in the early morning hours of July 29, 1954. "The Peanut Vendor" retakes were the final scenes filmed; a traditional wrap party followed.

The decision to shoot and insert Mama's showbiz tribute into a movie of already-epic length resulted in a challenging running time of well over three hours. The first preview of *A Star Is Born*, held in Huntington Park, California, on August 2, 1954, was an unqualified success. The second preview, held the following evening in Encino, California, was just as encouraging. Cukor noted in a letter to Moss Hart his surprise that small cuts had been attempted at Warner's behest. "He succeeded in muddying things up, making scenes pointless and incomprehensible—all this without losing any footage to speak of.…" Many of the cuts were restored at Cukor's behest. Cukor also noted that after the preview, my parents heard such comments as "Don't cut a single inch of it." Yet Cukor himself wished the film was shorter, "Neither the human mind nor the human ass can stand three and a half hours of concentration."[22]

Though Warner Bros. was still concerned about the film's length, Jack L. Warner encouraged my parents to indulge in a European holiday. He would join them and partially pay for their tour out of the anticipated profits, a reward for completing what every indication showed to be a hit film. Mama, however, had reservations about traveling to the French Riviera. As producer, she believed my father should have remained at his post in Burbank, overseeing the delicate editing process of a difficult movie, especially since Cukor had left the production. The gambling Lufts were still gambling, after the fact, with the picture's financial success. Clearly, my parents played a role in the movie's failure. My father and mother always felt the victim on this particular project, yet it seems obvious that their lack of involvement at this key moment shows their culpability in hindering what was supposed to be the major comeback vehicle of Mama's career. It's a shame they didn't stay in Hollywood and nurture their project just a little while longer, fight for it just a little bit harder. They should have. It shows they weren't equipped as producers.

As they celebrated the movie's completion, another celebration was taking place: my parents were expecting again. (The baby-to-be would be my younger brother, Joe, whose birth would play a part in the Oscar race in 1955.) Aiding the festive mood was my mother's face on the cover of *Life* magazine's September 13, 1954, issue in a photograph by Bob Willoughby.

Beneath the headline "Judy Garland Takes Off After an Oscar" was Mama's freckle-painted face in her "ragamuffin newsboy" costume (for the number "Lose That Long Face"); beneath that was the tag "Judy as a Gamin." The cover story inside heralded a "New Day for Judy: Garland's energy and talent create then overcome obstacles in *Star Is Born*." Photographer Sanford Roth visited the set for the magazine, documenting a few days in the life of a big Hollywood movie that was also a big-deal return for its star. The text accompanying the photo essay attributed the long shooting process to the star's perfectionism, frequent fatigue, "demands for new musical numbers," and "fiery temperament." The candid shots of Mama in motion and repose were combined with production stills, creating a superficially accurate portrait of an "imaginative, tireless, talented" star.[23]

Everything about this film seemed to demand special attention: first-class treatment, careful handling, and ramped-up hyperbole.

Everything about this film seemed to demand special attention: first-class treatment, careful handling, and ramped-up hyperbole. It had taken ten months to shoot; it encompassed the return of a beloved star; it was a hometown tale, an inside peek at the film industry. It was an epic of sorts, an intimate one, and a nontraditional musical in which every song had only one singer. At 196 minutes, it was the lengthiest major Hollywood movie since *Gone With the Wind* (1939), and the longest ever for Warner Bros. (*Gone With the Wind* had been successfully reissued that year, proving audiences were still willing to sit for lengthy films.) Late in the game, Cukor returned, and with his editor, Folmar Blangsted, worked diligently to trim fifteen minutes of running time. Believing Jack Warner had mismanaged the cutting, they smoothed out a few rough edges and cut the following brief scenes: a montage of Maine's big hit movies; Maine circling back to the Shrine in search of Esther; at the boardinghouse, Esther washing her hair; Maine's pirate movie being shot; Esther and Norman planning their beach house; and from "Born in a Trunk," the mother's death that was accompanied by "When My Sugar Walks Down the Street." This version, running 181 minutes, was the one that premiered and was shown in Hollywood, New York City, Chicago, and elsewhere until the middle of October.

—➤ • ⧼—

MY PARENTS RETURNED FROM THEIR THREE-WEEK EUROPEAN HOLIDAY JUST in time for the Hollywood premiere. As a result, advance publicity interviews with Mama were hard to come by. She was once again, unthinkingly, playing a game of roulette with the financial success of the picture as Dad stood by, enabling her. Still, the world premiere, held in Hollywood on September 29, 1954, was a smash. To label it a "gala" would have been an understatement—it was the social event of the year and makes a *Star Wars* premiere of today look like a simple industry gathering. At the RKO Pantages Theatre on Hollywood Boulevard, more than 20,000 fans collected through the day, eagerly awaiting Judy Garland and a Who's-Who swarm of celebrities to arrive for the 8:30 p.m. screening. The klieg-lit affair was an unconscious reenactment of the traffic-jammed, boisterous, camera-flashing crush of the movie's first moments at the "Night of the Stars" celebrity bash. The ABC radio network and its affiliate stations covered the proceedings all over the country. Local Los Angeles television station KTTV broadcast a "live" half-hour special statewide (with a portion of the live telecast airing simultaneously on NBC's *The Tonight Show* in New York City) as the stars exited their limousines, tuxedoed and gowned, and made their way through the throng. The host of the show, radio personality George Fisher, amped up expectations, calling the night "the greatest in the history of motion pictures." Desi Arnaz and Lucille Ball—obviously having already been treated to a special screening—scooped the critics. "It's the greatest!" Lucy shouted, over the noise.

Practically all of Hollywood turned out, from established stars like Clark Gable to hot young newcomers like James Dean. Over 250 celebrities parted the crowds, among them Lauren Bacall, Marlene Dietrich, Janet Leigh and Tony Curtis, Doris Day, Edward G. Robinson,

Elizabeth Taylor and Michael Wilding, Elia Kazan, Greer Garson, Debbie Reynolds, and Andy Devine (from *A Star Is Born*, 1937). The VIPs continued to flow into the theater: Danny Thomas, Mitzi Gaynor, Sophie Tucker, Jerry Lewis, Dean and Jeanne Martin, Cesar Romero, Gloria Grahame, Shelley Winters, Ann Sheridan, Joan Crawford, Alan Ladd, and Liberace with his mother. All of the major gossip columnists were in attendance: Louella Parsons, Hedda Hopper, Sheilah Graham, Harrison Carroll, and Earl Wilson. The star power was as present and potent as a night at the Academy Awards. The *Los Angeles Times*, in the next day's edition, described the evening: "There was never in modern days such mad, dizzying excitement in the forecourt of a theater, with such an array of glittering personalities." On the broadcast platform, George Jessel—the man who had swapped Gumm for Garland—muscled in to introduce Jack L. Warner and the star, whom he called "the great talent of our generation." Mama responded, "For me it's the most thrilling…I hope the picture is that good." Jessel pressed on, "Her husband and producer," eliciting from my modest father, "I'm proud to be a very small part of it." Warner joined in to hype: "Really the greatest opening in the history of my forty years in show business!" Assisting George Fisher when Jessel was otherwise engaged were three starlets, one of whom was Amanda Blake (best remembered as Miss Kitty on the television series *Gunsmoke*), who was a casualty of the cutting-room floor, playing in *A Star Is Born* someone called Susan Ettinger. The film's Jack Carson also fielded the surge of celebrities.[24]

A contract designer at RKO, Michael Woulfe, designed Mama's premiere ensemble. Months before, she had asked to borrow a suit from Jean Simmons that had caught her eye; the piece was one of Woulfe's, made for Simmons. The designer instead came up with a black velvet dress with a beaded white stand-up bateau collar encircling her neck. A small pillbox hat of beaded white satin almost completed the picture. Mama also requested a black fur muff large enough to conceal a handy flask of vodka—her nerve-steadier of choice, just as it had been on the set of the movie. Extravagant accolades passed all around as the film concluded

OPPOSITE: J. L. Warner, my mother, my father, George Cukor, and Warner Bros. distribution president Benjamin Kalmenson, attend the second "preview" of *A Star Is Born*, held at the Encino Theatre, Encino, California, August 1954.

ABOVE: My mother—looking jubilant—with my father arrive at the premiere of *A Star Is Born*. Jack L. Warner, who is facing my parents, is at left. OPPOSITE: The theater marquee of the RKO Pantages Theatre, 6233 Hollywood Boulevard, Hollywood, September 1954. The film boasted both Technicolor and CinemaScope.

at the Pantages Theatre. Mama was in Hollywood heaven, with more revelry to follow at the Cocoanut Grove at the Ambassador Hotel, where Jack Warner hosted a soiree for eight hundred guests titled "Night of Stars," with a menu of poached eggs benedict, chicken à la king (with pecan waffle), sirloin steak, ice cream, cake, coffee, and cocktails. My mother wasn't dieting that night. It was a time of happy celebration. Mama was in a state of rapture, and all the stars in attendance were lavishing praise on her and Dad. They were so happy to have successfully crossed the finish line. Enjoying the film with their peers, followed by the lavish Cocoanut Grove supper party, was one of the happiest nights of their lives.

ABOVE: My father gives my mother a kiss at the premiere party at the Cocoanut Grove. OPPOSITE, FROM TOP: Mama dances with Frank Sinatra at the premiere party at the Cocoanut Grove. Uncle Frank had recently enjoyed his own movie comeback with *From Here to Eternity* (1953). • Jack Carson, George Jessel, my mother, my father, and Jack Warner at the world premiere of *A Star Is Born* at the RKO Pantages Theatre, Hollywood, September 1954.

The double-venue premiere in Manhattan, on October 11, was another frenzied affair. Amid the chaos, Mama was surrounded by mounted police. At one point, she found herself standing next to a horse that lifted its tail and relieved itself right on the pavement. Not missing a beat, my mother did a double take and remarked, "Everyone's a critic."[25] She turned and marched into the theater in her stunning crimson gown with mink collar. New York City had been put in a receptive mood by Ed Sullivan, who had featured clips from the film (not standard practice in those days) on his variety show the night before. ABC television and NBC radio covered the arrivals, and scored the interviews. The ubiquitous George Jessel emceed the screening at the Paramount Theatre while announcer Martin Block served as emcee at the Victoria; the post-premiere party was held at the Waldorf Astoria. A few days later, there was another effusive premiere in Chicago. To my mother, the most important and touching outpouring of affection was the Hollywood event, where the elite had appeared in huge numbers, in her "hometown."

The initial reviews were ecstatic. Mama had hit her mark. *Time* was enthusiastic: "An expert vaudeville performance was to be expected from Judy; to find her a dramatic actress, as well, is the real surprise." The magazine considered the film "a stunning comeback" and "just about the greatest one-woman show in modern movie history."[26] In a mixed review, Edwin Schallert of the *Los Angeles Times* described Mama's performance as "overstressed," and "potentially a target for strong critical resistance," presumably because the film was too long and "overburdened" with trying to prove itself, and he felt its emotional scenes were forced. But Schallert was still swept into the razzle-dazzle, admitting the musical "put a brilliantly shining crown upon the dark-tressed head of Judy Garland....Here was her super-picture."[27] Critics could not deny the picture's grandeur. In the *New York Times*, Bosley Crowther gushed, "It is something to see, this *Star Is Born*."[28] The editor-in-chief of *Variety*, Abel Green, predicted, "Boffola box office," and went on to note the early grosses in various markets (in 1950s *Variety*

OPPOSITE: The New York City premiere of *A Star Is Born* was held simultaneously at the Paramount Theatre and the Victoria Theatre, October 1954. My father puffs on a cigarette at left while my mother beams at the throng gathered upon her arrival at the Paramount in Times Square.

vernacular): "terrif, whopping, sockeroo." Bravos went to George Cukor ("No one surpasses Mr. Cukor at handling this sort of thing"); James Mason (a fine "portrait of a tormented ego"); Moss Hart ("has smoothly modernized...the sweet and touching love story"); and all who fashioned "one of the grandest heartbreak dramas that has drenched the screen in years."[29] And, they set it to music.

Because her reputation had been somewhat tarnished by her later years at MGM, she was particularly gratified that her peers, the critics, and the industry as a whole now embraced her and *A Star Is Born.*

My mother was thrilled by the overwhelmingly positive reception. Because her reputation had been somewhat tarnished by her later years at MGM, she was particularly gratified that her peers, the critics, and the industry as a whole now embraced her and *A Star Is Born.* She had cut her losses, started fresh at a new studio (with a new husband-producer in her corner), and had succeeded on a grand scale. Mama was officially back, and she was the toast of the town. And she didn't have to grovel or beg for a second chance. Like Frank Sinatra, she did it her way. It must have been one of the most rewarding periods in Mama's career.

Most who saw the original cut of the film, running three hours and one minute, were not bothered by its length. But for some, 181 minutes of Judy Garland's talent was a little too much. Playwright and composer Noël Coward, a great friend of hers, nevertheless wrote in his private diary, "Every song was attenuated to such a length that I thought I was going mad.... One in par-

Mama appears very happy (and very pregnant with my brother Joe) with Marlon Brando and Edmond O'Brien at the Hollywood Foreign Press Association's Golden Globe Awards, February 1955. As this candid photo illustrates, Mama was always the life of the party and all eyes were invariably on her. She won Best Actress (Musical or Comedy) for *A Star Is Born* at the banquet; Brando won Best Actor in a Motion Picture (Drama) for *On the Waterfront* (1954); and O'Brien won Best Supporting Actor in a Motion Picture (Drama) for *The Barefoot Contessa* (1954).

ticular, 'Born in a Trunk,' started brilliantly but by the time it was over and we had endured montage after montage and repetition after repetition, I found myself wishing that dear enchanting Judy was at the bottom of the sea."[30] Coward, known as "The Master," was not alone in his reaction to Mama's film. Many found it overwhelming, intense, and exhausting. It was also extremely long. As early as mid-October, dissatisfied theater owners and operators complained that they could only screen the movie three times per day due to its running time. They wanted a box-office-friendly blockbuster that they could unreel four times a day. Jack Warner heard the grumblings, but was not inclined to axe thirty minutes out of a picture in which he was personally invested, a film of which he was truly proud. But at the Warner offices in New York City—from which Jack's elder brother Harry called all the shots as president of Warner Bros.—the word was "cut!"

The brothers Warner had always had an adversarial relationship, Harry being the intimidating force over the otherwise confidant and controlling Jack. Other strategies might have worked, namely turning the film into a road-show event with higher ticket prices. Harry would not entertain any compromises. The exhibitors wanted four shows a day instead of three. Harry was adamant on the cuts that Jack knew would gut the film—not only at that time, but forever. Barrie Richardson of the Warner Bros. sales department selected what was to be cut, and film editor Folmar Blangsted carried out the work without the consultation of George Cukor, who was in India at that time directing *Bhowani Junction* (1956). The studio eliminated the unwanted material from the original negative and discarded the excised footage. Additionally, all 200 full-length prints in existence were cut at the various film exchanges to conform to the new, shortened 154-minute length for wide release. I've even heard that, in a few instances, Warner Bros. sent instructions for the film to be cut by projectionists. It's like the L. P. Hartley line, "The past is a foreign country; they do things differently there." It's insanity thinking about it now. No projectionist would take a pair of scissors to a Spielberg movie. The entire job was botched. They did surgery on a healthy patient without anesthesia, removing major organs and expecting the patient to survive.

OPPOSITE: Mama in a moment of reflection during a rehearsal. Photo by Sanford Roth.

These film trims were sent back to Warner Bros. where they were destroyed. Incredibly, Warner Bros. didn't retain a single print of the original, full-length 181-minute version that was seen and reviewed in Los Angeles, New York City, Chicago, and elsewhere to great critical acclaim. Harry's edict failed to please anyone, but he seemed to take pleasure in invading his little brother's territory. But in winning the battle, he lost the war, the spoils of which destroyed *A Star Is Born* at the box office.

The new version, at 154 minutes, eliminated entire scenes. In chronological order:

1) Esther says good-bye to the band at the bus the morning after Maine's peptalk.

2) Maine, half-asleep, bundled into a town car to be taken to his movie's location.

3) Esther washes her hair at the Oleander Arms.

4) Oliver Niles on the telephone to Maine's director.

5) Maine on the telephone to his assistant, trying to locate Esther.

6) Esther at her rooming house, getting news of a singing gig.

7) Esther sings for Trinidad Coconut Oil Shampoo.

8) Esther in uniform at a drive-in, talking to Danny in a telephone booth.

9) Esther offers a customer "everything in the place, all burgered!"

10) Maine at Oleander Arms with the landlady.

11) Maine, with Lola Lavery, hears, then sees, the Trinidad commercial on television.

12) Maine finds Esther at the rooming house.

13) Maine and Esther drive to the sneak preview.

These are severe first-act cuts that explode the narrative into fragments, leaving the audience wondering what they missed. The revised story line jumps from Esther telling her friend Danny that she is quitting the band's tour, to the studio makeup department where Esther is being readied for her screen test. The second-act omissions are fewer but no less damaging, because they are two song cuts: the recording session of "Here's What I'm Here For," the setting for Norman's marriage proposal, and the "Lose That Long Face" production number. "Born in a Trunk" survived, as well as "Someone at Last," but the scissoring left the first act without its logic and its emotional center. It also left first-time viewers in the dark.

Mama was in shock when informed about the extent of the cuts. She told Dad, "Do something!" He was powerless as he didn't have final cut over the picture. Mama felt the rug had been pulled out from under her. That safety net that she craved, once again, had disappeared. Mama relied on my father for certain things, and this was one of them. She couldn't do it all. There was simply no time. My mother managed a lot of living and accomplishment in her relatively short life. Mama received all her training by simply getting up there and performing on the stage and later as one of the "Meglin Kiddies" (a children's dance school.) Later, she had great teachers, coaches, and mentors at MGM. The only thing they failed to teach her were the skills of a CPA and attorney. Why would anyone expect her to understand the business side of making movies? That's what my father was supposed to look after. Dad, feeling betrayed, blamed Jack Warner. Liza, then eight years old, remembers the night our mother found out about the massive cuts, including "Lose That Long Face." Mama came up to her room in tears and said, "They just don't care."[31] It soon became even worse. Suddenly, lawsuits were threatened and pursued against my father, in separate actions by Harry and Jack Warner, each claiming my father had wrangled loans from them in the course of making the picture. The dollar amounts were negligible to the mogul brothers, but the point seemed to be the shaming of Sid Luft, whom they had both come to personally loathe. (The two brothers also despised each other with an enmity for the ages. In 1956, the two remaining Warner brothers sold 90 percent of their Warner Bros. stock to a syndicate, but the crafty Jack Warner used the sale as a scheme to rid himself of Harry, as he repurchased the shares and then some in a secret deal. Jack L. Warner emerged president of Warner Bros. with Harry out of a job.)

Dad had gambled once too often with the big guys, and lost again. After a promising start, the very bad word of mouth for the cut version scuttled hopes for the movie's chances. Despite

the buildup, the critical praise, and the virtually unanimous approval of the original edit, the butchered version of *A Star Is Born* was a financial failure. The fallout was more than just a disappointment or an economical loss; it was a personal failure for Judy Garland—one from which her film stardom would never fully recover.

Warner Bros. did not mount an aggressive Oscar campaign for Mama or *A Star Is Born*. But there was still a glimmer of hope: the Oscar nominations were announced in the spring of 1955. The final five in contention for Best Actress were Dorothy Dandridge (*Carmen Jones*), Audrey Hepburn (*Sabrina*), Grace Kelly (*The Country Girl*), Jane Wyman (*Magnificent Obsession*) and Judy Garland. *A Star Is Born* received five other nominations, a large number, considering the financial disaster the film had become. The recognition had been part of Mama's comeback dream all along. Though she had won the Juvenile Award miniature statuette for her work in *The Wizard of Oz*, Mama craved the cachet a "real" full-sized Oscar would bring with it—a heavy, gold-plated certification of respect, even love, from an industry that had brought mixed blessings into her life.

On the evening of March 28, however, Mama was showing signs of premature labor. Hurried to Cedars of Lebanon

Mama prepares backstage for a concert at the Greek Theatre, a 5,800-seat music venue in Los Angeles, June 1957. This was my mother's last stop on a nine-week tour. It was her first appearance in Los Angeles since her spectacular "comeback" at the Los Angeles Philharmonic Auditorium five years earlier and broke the previous box office record.

163

Hospital, on the eastern edge of Beverly Hills, she gave birth at 2:16 a.m. to her third child and first son by Caesarean section. He weighed five pounds, eight ounces, and was given the name Joseph Wiley Luft. Two of the biggest events in her life bumped up against each other. The Academy Awards ceremony was to be held on the 30th, and Mama was still in the hospital.

In a 1957 article published in *McCall's*, my mother recounted her Oscar night experience:

> There I was, weak and exhausted. . . . As I lay there in bed, the door burst open and in came a flock of TV technicians. I already had a television set in my room, but they dragged in two more huge ones. When I asked why two sets, I was told that I would have to talk back and forth to Bob Hope, who was master of ceremonies at the awards, and they couldn't take a chance on one of the sets not working properly. Then they strung wires all around the room, put a microphone under the sheets and frightened the poor nurses almost to death by saying, "If you pull up the Venetian blinds before they say 'Judy Garland' we'll kill you."
>
> Outside the window I could see the cameramen on the tower getting ready to focus on me in bed. Then someone turned on the TV set and Bob Hope came on. We listened to the whole ceremony, the excitement building up. Then Bob announced the winning actress. It was Grace Kelly.
>
> I didn't have time to be disappointed, I was fascinated by the reactions of the men. They got mad at me for losing and started lugging all their stuff out of the room. They didn't even say good night.[32]

Kelly was a newcomer who had been working in Hollywood only four years, as opposed to Mama's twenty. Good friend Lauren Bacall was with her in the hospital that Monday night, and wrote later that she was gracious in defeat, saying her baby boy was much more important than any award. Bacall remembered:

The big night came and we were all gathered around our sets praying—and Judy lost. She carried it off beautifully, saying her son, Joey, was more important than any Oscar could be, but she was deeply disappointed—and hurt. It confirmed her belief that the industry was against her. She knew it was then or never. Instinctively, all her friends knew the same. Judy wasn't like any other performer. There was so much emotion involved in her career—in her life—it was always all or nothing. And though she put on a hell of a front, this was one more slap in the face. She was bitter about it, and, for that matter, all closest to her were.[33]

Disbelief and outrage mixed with support were expressed publicly and privately. Lucille Ball had spoken to the national television audience on the night of the Hollywood premiere, declaring, "Judy and James and George Cukor and everybody else in this picture are going to take all the Academy Awards they have. I'm sure of it!" Groucho Marx sent what became a famous telegram, "This is the biggest robbery since Brinks."[34] Hedda Hopper maintained it had been the closest race in Oscar history (short of a tie), just seven voters separating the two nominees, "You know who those seven votes were, don't you? They belonged to those bastards in the front office of MGM."[35] Hopper was referring to the residual resentments at the studio regarding Mama's final years there. Garland biographer Christopher Finch is of the opinion that the votes against the temperamental star and producer were a "reprimand" for the profligate production.[36] George Cukor believed, "The picture is totally fragmented. I think it accounts for why Judy Garland didn't win the Academy Award."[37] Just as Norman Maine back-handed Vicki Lester on the stage at the Academy Awards, so the Academy of Motion Picture Arts and Sciences seemed to slap Judy Garland, in one of the greatest upsets in Oscar history.

A Star Is Born garnered other nominations: James Mason for Actor in a Leading Role; Gene Allen, Malcolm Bart, Irene Sharaff, and George James Hopkins for Art Direction/Set Decoration, Color; and Mary Ann Nyberg, Jean Louis, and Irene Sharaff for Costume Design, Color. Ray Heindorf's music scoring was nominated, as was Mama's signature song from the film, "The Man That Got Away" by Ira Gershwin and Harold Arlen. But the award went to "Three Coins in the Fountain" by Jule Styne and Sammy Cahn, a win even the composers thought misguided, when compared to the Gershwin/Arlen masterwork. The Hollywood Foreign Press Association's annual award ceremony, the Golden Globes, held earlier in the year, were staged at the Cocoanut Grove, a venue that seemed to dog Mama's steps. She and Mason were named Best Actress and Actor, Musical or Comedy. Best Picture, Musical or Comedy, however, was awarded to *Carmen Jones*. Mama was nominated for Best Foreign Actress by the British Film Academy. George Cukor won the Directors Guild of America Award, while the National Board of Review named the film to its official Top Ten of 1954. The New York Film Critics Circle revealed both Mama and James as second-place Best Actress and Actor.

Movie offers and project pitches didn't stop after Mama lost the Oscar. *The Three Faces of Eve* (1957) was sent to her first, but

Mama greets her fans at Carnegie Hall, April 23, 1961. This was Mama's most famous concert performance, and the album made live from the event was her greatest recording success.

she and my father quickly turned it down, even though she thought she could play the hell out of it. Joanne Woodward benefited from Mama's noncommittals, unavailability, withdrawn offers, and delayed projects. George Cukor disowned the movie, yet he accepted Jack Warner's offer to direct another musical film—a full-fledged musical classic, at that—*My Fair Lady* (1964). It won eight Academy Awards, including Best Picture. Go figure.

As a person and a performer, my mother moved on, determined to be victorious, though my father continued to play the victim. After his failure as a producer, he blamed friends as well as foes. Mama, always in need of funds, optimistically turned to television guest spots and solo programs. The concert stage and nightclubs also appeared viable again, thanks to the boost the movie gave her name on a marquee. Dad remained by her side, battle after battle. Mama could not know that her next film was years away, and she had three children—and a husband—to support. (My father acted as her manager when he wasn't betting on the ponies at Hollywood Park or Santa Anita.) At the end of 1954, Mama signed a one-year contract with MCA for across-the-board representation. The agency would be in the Judy Garland business despite the crash-and-burn of her go-for-broke comeback movie, fielding requests for recording sessions, television appearances, live performances, and motion pictures.

A recording contract with Capitol Records, prompted by strong sales figures for the *A Star Is Born* soundtrack, was put together, and lasted through 1964, placing my mother on the same roster as Frank Sinatra and Nat "King" Cole.

One year later, Mama and MCA agreed to another five years. A recording contract with Capitol Records, prompted by strong sales figures for the *A Star Is Born* soundtrack, was put together, and lasted through 1964, placing my mother on the same roster as Frank Sinatra and Nat "King" Cole. In March 1955, Warner Bros. and Transcona Enterprises dissolved their multipicture deal, with *A Star Is Born* being the only film made under the agreement. Undeterred, the following month, my father announced a seven-city tour, to begin that summer, of *The Judy Garland Show*, a three-hour concert with special guests, climaxing with a two-month engagement at the Winter Garden in New York. The travel, city to city, reminded her of her childhood and adolescent years as a little vaudevillian. The stage fright that sometimes overtook her persisted, but a change occurred in her reaction. She fell in love with her audience.

My mother's dependence on prescription drugs, the legacy left her by ill-advised and careless handlers during her contract years at MGM, continued to plague her. Benzedrine would spike her energy in the morning and throughout the day; Seconal would induce late-night sleep. A flask of vodka was nearly always available. Dad knew that, not long after Joey's birth, she had been acquiring and using her prescription medication in alarming doses once again. He searched her bedroom, finding pills behind books, under the rugs, in her slippers and the hems of dresses, anywhere quickly stashed and easily retrieved. It has to be remembered that the prescriptions that were causing her dependency were *from a doctor*, so, in Mama's mind, they were supposed to help her. Her mind and body craved these medicines and no one knew how to stop those cravings. It was called the "mysterious illness." My father did his best. He fell in love with the brilliantly talented and funny person that Mama was, but the baggage that came with her stardom, I don't think he was equipped to handle. Alcoholics Anonymous existed during this time, but how could someone like Judy Garland attend AA meetings and remain anonymous? Dad tried to control Mama's needs with low doses, but conceded, "The fact is that she was married to the drugs before she met me, and she never really got divorced."[38]

An offer came from CBS—$100,000 for a ninety-minute prime-time spectacular. The resultant broadcast, on September 24, 1955, drew 44 million viewers to their televisions. Three more specials were contracted, but just one live broadcast (on April 8, 1956) materialized, due to disputes over content and issues with Mama's ever-fluctuating weight. My parents set their sights on Las Vegas, where her show at the New Frontier set a box office record of $55,000 per week.

The hotel management encouraged her to stay longer, but Mama moved on, with renewed confidence, to the Palace in New York, where Dad marveled at her elevated mood. But a second Vegas appearance at the Flamingo at the end of 1957 went badly, and Mama forfeited $100,000 by cutting short the three-week engagement. And so it went—disaster always following closely on the heels of triumph. The Lufts lived an itinerant showbiz life. They were away more than at home, and in search of the next lucrative deal as their lavish lifestyle had them constantly in debt.

Tensions mounted in this marriage between a free-spirited star and her hustling husband. Starting at age ten, Liza would tightly cover her ears to block out the vitriol hurled from both sides in my parents' titanic wrangles. I remember when everything started to unravel at home. They would fight, separate, then reunite in an ongoing pattern. After a life-threatening health crisis put Mama in the Doctors Hospital in Manhattan for seven weeks in late 1959 (she was suffering from cirrhosis of the liver but it was explained to the press at the time as hepatitis) she decided that, in the summer of 1960, we would move to London, where she could enjoy a lucrative concert career there and in Europe. England made my mother feel safe because they loved her so much and it was a new beginning. We lived in a lovely house on King's Road in the Chelsea neighborhood of West London that belonged to British film director Carol Reed. It was a magical period for the entire family because we were chasing a dream of "Let's start all over again." Mama kept an eye on American politics from abroad, as a new young candidate, John F. Kennedy, emerged to lead the pack. Mama supported his campaign, considering him a friend and, over time, a confidante.

The following year, Mama was in New York City and my parents were separated frequently. One of my father's favorite memories during this period involves *A Star Is Born*. On February 25, 1961, the first New York City television broadcast of the film took place on WROC-TV. At 11:15 p.m., when the film ended, Dad—alone in his hotel—received a phone call from the hotel lobby. It was Mama's chauffeur. "This is Miss Garland's chauffeur," the man said. "Miss Garland is here, in her car, and she would like to see you."

Dad went downstairs and outside, in the back of the limousine, was Mama with a bottle of champagne in an ice bucket with two glasses. "Hi, darling," she said. "You watched the picture?" He nodded that he had. "Wasn't it great?" she asked. "You produced a great picture, Sid." My father replied, "Judy, it was your picture and you were great in it and it's great to see you again." Her voice breaking with emotion, she said, "Let's celebrate." The two of them did just that, at the El Morocco nightclub in New York City.[39]

Dad took leave of his management duties when Freddie Fields, until recently at MCA, promised Mama a career, not just one-shot jobs. A gentleman with a plan, he secured for her a U.S. concert tour, a new CBS television special, and a role in *Judgment at Nuremberg*, Stanley Kramer's message picture, heavy with prestige. Mama would be part of a large all-star ensemble, playing a victim of Nazi persecution. Her three scenes, comprising just fifteen minutes of screen time, packed a punch, landing her another Oscar nomination, this time for Best Supporting Actress. Although she didn't win, the Academy Award nomination meant a great deal to her as it was a dramatic role in an important film. The concert tour was a stellar success, with two performances at Carnegie Hall being the highlights of Mama's concert bookings that year, the recording of which held the number-one position for thirteen weeks and remained on *Billboard's* top 40 for seventy-three weeks. *Judy at Carnegie Hall* later won four Grammy Awards, including Best Female Vocalist and Album of the Year. The CBS television special, with Frank Sinatra and Dean Martin, was a ratings smash, solidly besting its direct competition, NBC's *Bonanza*. These singular victories solidified, even magnified, the legend that Judy Garland began to embody: the lady down for the count, arising, not just to fight on, but to win. She was back on top again.

The songs she sang onstage were personal metaphors, enriching her story: "Over the Rainbow," "Get Happy," "The Man That Got Away." The Judy juggernaut was a phenomenon from 1961 through mid-1963. She was everywhere: in the movies, on television, on records, touring the country. It seemed she had finally found her sweet spot in material, medium, and audience. However, the veneer of good fortune and high spirits was beginning to crack.

Mama loaned her golden voice to Mewsette, an animated Parisian cat, singing five new songs by Harold Arlen and E. Y. Harburg in *Gay Purr-ee* (1962), a charming feature-length animated musical. Mewsette and company had only minor box-office success, with *Newsweek* observing the film was targeting "a hitherto undiscovered audience—the fey four-year-old of recherché taste."[40] Another Stanley Kramer production, *A Child Is Waiting* (1963), this one directed by John Cassavetes, was a trial for everyone involved. Even with Burt Lancaster costarring, audiences stayed away from the small picture with a big message about children with intellectual disabilities.

Before leaving New York for London to make *I Could Go on Singing*, my parents had an ultimate confrontation at the Stanhope Hotel on Fifth Avenue. Mama would insist that the dispute involved a physical assault, which is untrue. Their verbal attacks on each other were often vicious, but my father rarely laid a hand on my mother. She, Liza, Joey, and I were tucked into two limousines at the time, about to be whisked to the airport. Mama hated the script waiting for her in London, telling the story of a brilliant, yet very troubled singer—art was cuddling up too close to life. Friend and costar Dirk Bogarde was her protector, acting as a liaison between Mama and the producers and director Ronald Neame. But after one day on the set, armed with her ever-present pills, my mother attempted suicide. As with all her suicide attempts, it was a cry for help in a moment of dark despair. Mama's lows were very low, just as her highs were higher than anyone's. Mama was the most positive human being I've ever known. She always looked at the glass as being half-full. When at her lowest, she would pick herself up, dust herself off, and start all over again. She always looked for the silver lining. The problem was that silver has a tendency to tarnish.

Once filming resumed on *I Could Go on Singing*, the recovering star and Bogarde tried their hand at improvising, an especially effective strategy for the famous scene in the hospital where the singer is backed into a corner. Bogarde later wrote that Mama, in one long take, had gone "from black farce right through to black tragedy, a cadenza of pain and suffering, of bald, unvarnished truth."[41] This sequence is the breakdown-in-the-dressing-room scene in *A Star Is Born* all over again, minus the straw hat and freckles. Mama, of course, sang the title song by Arlen and Harburg, but even that did little to help the film find an audience. After this project,

Mama with Dirk Bogarde in the famous hospital sequence from *I Could Go on Singing* (1963). The sequence was inspired by the breakdown scene in *A Star Is Born* and was captured in one take.

she found herself once again strapped financially and damaged professionally. Returning to the concert stage and the nightclub circuit was her best option. The Sahara Hotel in Las Vegas, making her feel respected and supported, adjusted her show time to 2:30 a.m. to accommodate her night-owl habits. Mama still sold out the house.

She also became a favorite talk-show guest, not only singing, but telling bawdy, raucous stories from her vaudeville days and her tenure at MGM, casually dropping the names of Mickey

Rooney, Lana Turner, or Orson Welles. She was proving herself to be one of classic Hollywood's most entertaining raconteurs, her quick wit matched by her gifts for physical comedy—she would often stand up to deliver her punch lines. Audiences adored her. Her very first television talk-show appearance was on *The Jack Paar Program*, broadcast December 7, 1962, when she was promoting *Gay Pur-ee*. She sang "Little Drops of Rain" and "Paris Is a Lonely Town" before sitting with Paar for a hilarious chat. This lady was approaching the status of national treasure, if one who carried the baggage of her not-so-secret problems everywhere she landed.

Freddie Fields and his associate, David Begelman, capitalizing on the impressive ratings for Mama's special, put together a package for all three networks to consider: a Judy Garland television variety series of twenty-six one-hour shows. CBS got on board swiftly, agreeing to pay the star $25,000 to $30,000 per show. After the network had made its target profit, they would allow her to take full ownership of the tapes and any further profits from their syndication. The show would be rehearsed and taped at CBS Television City in Hollywood. Mama was thrilled; she could rent or buy a house for her family to live in, and be home to tuck us in at night (except on evenings of taping). She could finally leave the hotels to the tourists, and make some real money. Plus, she could welcome and work with the biggest stars and the newest talents. She could be funny, be charming, and sing, sing, sing.

The Judy Garland Show first aired on September 29, 1963, in the deadly 9:00 p.m. slot against *Bonanza*. The series started promisingly. Mama, slimmer than she had been in years, attractive, and glamorous, clearly enjoyed hosting her friends, appreciating their talents, and sharing hers. Her first guest was none other than her closest MGM colleague and friend, Mickey Rooney, although the first episode to air was the seventh show, featuring her good friend Donald O'Connor. Unfortunately, CBS president James Aubrey was not a Judy Garland fan; the deal was made just before he assumed his position. Instead of supporting *The Judy Garland Show* and nurturing its success, Aubrey lost interest when it became clear it was not going to beat *Bonanza* in the Nielsen ratings. The show went through three different produc-

OPPOSITE: Mama with guest Barbra Streisand sing a "Hooray for Love" medley on the *The Judy Garland Show* (1963). The show, the ninth episode of the series, was recorded and aired in October 1963.

ers (George Schlatter, Norman Jewison, and Bill Colleran) and format changes. Mama tried to stay above the fray, saying, when questioned about her struggling show, that television was completely new to her, and that she would leave the tinkering to the experts. Her skills would have been better suited to a less scripted, more improvisational format, instead of being put in the position of ringmaster. A favorite segment was "Born in a Trunk," a reference to *A Star Is Born*, where she would reminisce from her showbiz past as the springboard for a solo.

One episode, however, remains an example of what was right about the show at its best. A new sensation named Barbra Streisand was the guest, and she not only sang two beautiful solos—"Bewitched" and "Down with Love"—but made beautiful music with my mother. Barbra performed one of her signature songs, "Happy Days Are Here Again" in counterpoint to Mama's "Get Happy." In the footage, it's clear to see that Mama was a "toucher," placing a hand frequently on Barbra's arm, or leaning in close, shoulder to shoulder, as if trying to make contact, express affection, or just plain hold on for security and assurance. The drop-by of Ethel Merman was an inspiration: three generations in admiration, sizing each other up. My mother's solo spot at the show's end capped the episode with a simple communion between artist and audience.

John F. Kennedy's assassination occurred during a hiatus in the show's production. Upon returning to the studio, Mama and her producer decided that a song in tribute to the late president would serve as the climactic moment of the next show that aired. In heartfelt pain over the nation's loss, as well as her personal loss of a friend, Mama delivered a touching rendition of "The Battle Hymn of the Republic."

The series limped along through the season, but Aubrey seemed determined to see it fail. In January 1964, he publicly announced the cancellation of *The Judy Garland Show*, leaving Mama and her team to finish their commitment with a black cloud hanging over them. The sudden, publicized axing was uncalled for, even vicious, but Mama soldiered on, turning the final show (broadcast on March 29) into a solo concert of her favorite crowd-pleasers, new and old. As she so often did, my mother put on a brave public face. But, like the box-office failure of *A Star Is Born*, she

OPPOSITE: Mama, flanked by me and my brother Joe, as she prepares to open her third and final engagement at the Palace Theatre, New York City, July 1967.

never fully recovered from this high-profile and costly setback. Just like the film, Mama was told what she wanted to hear: She was to be safe. This was her new creative home and it led down the yellow brick road. She was going to be great. This would provide her financial independence.

Before the series was shut down, my parents made an attempt at a reconciliation—more Dad's doing than hers as David Begelman, the ambitious but duplicitous associate of Freddie Fields, was attempting to control her life. Begelman had been largely responsible for developing the series, but my suspicious father arranged an audit of the books and discovered that Begelman had embezzled nearly $300,000 from his wife's accounts and left her income tax unpaid. She placed the blame on the wrong man, however, excusing the loss as minor (it wasn't) and closing the door on Sid Luft. Mama was in debt once again, hopes for security dashed, and facing an uncertain future.

Never, it seems, was Mama very long without a male companion. She focused for a while on thirty-five-year-old actor Mark Herron, whom she met at a New Year's Eve party as 1963 made way for 1964. By this time, my mother had added Tuinal to her pharmaceutical inventory. When landing at the Sydney airport for a minitour in Australia, her entire stash was confiscated, causing a mad dash by Herron to replace it. The tour itself was an ordeal: the love that was showered on her in Sydney was eclipsed by derision in Melbourne, when the concert began extremely late. She overdosed in Hong Kong (on Tuinal), leaving her comatose in the hospital. Premature reporting claimed that she had died. Herron at her side, Mama continued pushing herself on from concert to concert, bouncing back after crashing flat.

My parents' divorce was final on May 19, 1965, leaving my mother free to marry Mark Herron in November at the Little Church of the West in Las Vegas. The couple were separated a year later. Herron maintained that he still loved her. I was thirteen at this tumultuous time, when our family life was crumbling to pieces. The burden fell to Liza, in New York City, to become a mother to her own mother, seeing her through the worst, and hoping for the best. Joey and I were also on high alert, loving our mother but fearing her next self-destructive cycle. One day, I whispered to my father, "Daddy, I've got Mama right here. Right here in the throat." I had an inkling that I possessed something of Mama's great talent, but I was fearful of the monster that might come with it. Did being her daughter doom me to the unhappiness she faced?

The hoopla surrounding the film version of Jacqueline Susann's best-selling 1966 novel *Valley of the Dolls* (1967) included the announcement that Judy Garland had been cast as Helen Lawson, the Broadway musical star, tough-as-nails broad, and ultimate survivor. For the juicy role, Mama would be paid $75,000 for ten days' work and ten minutes of screen time. Twentieth Century Fox rolled out the red carpet, but Mama, a hellion of few equals when feeling insecure, couldn't summon up the same cruel fire before the camera, and was let go. The studio permitted her to take one outfit and paid half of her salary. She chose a Travilla-designed pantsuit, heavily encrusted with beads and sequins, which she put to frequent use in concerts and personal appearances. Susan Hayward replaced her in the movie and wore the suit, exactly re-created.

Mama made the rounds of the 1960s television guest circuit, appearing on *The Hollywood Palace, The Ed Sullivan Show, The Merv Griffin Show*, and *The Mike Douglas Show*. On *The Dick Cavett Show* for the first time, on December 16, 1968, she looked like an abused doll, tiny and a bit raggedy next to the large and robust Lee Marvin. Six months before, on *The Tonight Show*, she had conversed brightly with Johnny Carson, and looked slim and vital; even somehow taller.

Fortunately, at this critical juncture, Mama secured an engagement at The Talk of the Town, the nightclub in the old London Hippodrome, at $6,000 per week. But before she left New York City for England, she happened to strike up a close friendship with Mickey Deans, the night manager of the Manhattan discotheque Arthur. Mama impulsively spoke of love as they flew to London in December 1968. They wed on March 15, 1969, in a quick civil ceremony not unlike the one that united Esther Blodgett and Ernest Sidney Gubbins. She was counting on Deans (born DeVinko) to tell her what to do, to fix her, since he seemed to be proficient at many things, one of them attaining access to the medication to which she was now deeply addicted. He was her miracle guy. He bolstered her enough to engage in a successful Scandinavian tour with Johnnie Ray that followed the Talk of the Town appearances. The dates in Stockholm, Malmo, and Copenhagen were applauded and praised extravagantly. As unhealthy as Mama was at this phase of her life, she still had what it took to wow a crowd.

Upon their return, the Deans rented a Chelsea Mews house, but it didn't take long for the inevitable downward spiral to manifest. Mickey was preoccupied—other things to do, other places to be. She had stopped eating and her brittle, starved body was more fragile than ever. Early on June 22, a Sunday, Mama locked herself in the bathroom, which she often did, but did not answer Mickey's knock on the door, or respond when he repeatedly called out her name. He scrambled outside and to the roof to let himself in through the window, but it was too late. My mother had slipped away. When he finally found her, she was slumped over and lifeless—and apparently had been for hours—the victim of a barbiturate overdose. (Mama had taken another dose of Seconal to enable her to sleep until morning.) Coroner Gavin Thurston wrote in his report that her death was accidental.

As much as Liza, Joey, Dad, and I loved her (and as much as she loved us), we were unable to save Judy Garland from herself. Toward the end, she needed constant caretaking, super-vision, and reassurance, but somehow, I always thought she would pull through. I never believed her life would end so suddenly, without any of her family present. For a long time, I blamed myself for not being there. We all did. But now I see that it was inevitable. If it hadn't happened that night, it would have happened soon thereafter. Her addictions, her demons had already taken away the mother of my early childhood memories, and now it had taken her away com-pletely. For me, my sister, and my brother, the shock and the loss were almost unbearable.

My mother's body was flown to New York, then taken to the Frank E. Campbell Funeral Chapel on the east side of Manhattan, where a public viewing would take place. A somber line formed, and grew, as over 20,000 fans and friends filed by the glass-enclosed coffin early Thursday afternoon, June 26, into Friday morning, to pay their respects and bid her farewell. The simple service commencing at one o'clock was spontaneously accompanied by the sound of Judy Garland singing from radios and portable record players outside, on the steps, and down the street. My sister, Liza, my brother Joe, and I, were joined by Mickey Deans to represent the family. Ray Bolger, Lauren Bacall, Kay Thompson, Harold Arlen, and my father were among those in attendance. (Mickey Rooney appeared briefly that morning, but did not stay for the service.) The Reverend Peter A. Delaney conducted the Episcopal service. "Here's to Us" and Mama's personal tribute to President Kennedy, "The Battle Hymn of the Republic," resounded through the room. James Mason delivered the eulogy. Standing in front of a blanket of yellow roses covering the coffin, he spoke of his *Star Is Born* costar, his colleague, and his friend.

> I traveled in her orbit only for a little while but it was an exciting while, and one during which it seemed that the joys in her life outbalanced the miseries. The little girl whom I knew, who had a little curl in the middle of her forehead, when she was good she was not only very, very good, she was the most sympathetic, the funniest, the sharpest and the most stimulating woman I ever knew. She was a lady who gave so much and richly, both to her vast audience who she entertained and to the friends around her whom she loved, that there was no currency in which to repay her. And she needed to be repaid, she needed devotion and love beyond the resources of any of us.[42]

Since I first caught it on late-night television, it took me a few more viewings to understand why *A Star Is Born* is so special, and why it was my mother's favorite of all her films. Now I see: it is her movie all the way. The whole thing—every song, every line of dialogue—is tailor-made to showcase her specific talents, quirks, and endearing qualities. The film is also deliberately self-referential to her own life and career. The catch in her throat when she belts the climactic notes in "The Man That Got Away." Her distinctive, musical laugh when she spots herself in the mirror in Norman's dressing room, her face slathered with cold cream. The sparkle in her eyes when she wipes her tears and opens her arms wide, grinning in her straw hat. These moments are so Mama, so quintessentially Judy Garland. It's her moment to shine. And in this film perhaps, more than any other, her spirit does shine on.

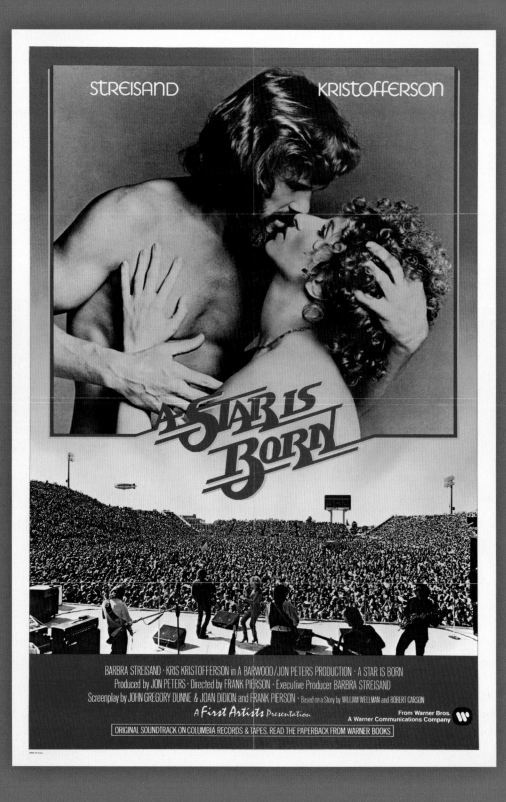

Chapter Three

BARBRA STREISAND'S
A STAR IS BORN
(1976)

WHILE SCREENWRITER MOSS HART CONCEIVED THE GEORGE CUKOR-Judy Garland version of *A Star Is Born* as a showcase for its star that would lead to a cinematic comeback, reestablishing Garland's stature as a top box-office draw, the Barbra Streisand remake would take one of the biggest box-office draws of the 1970s and turn her from being merely a star into a *super*star. The 1976 update would switch the setting from the glitz of Tinseltown to the gritty world of contemporary rock, and would delve into the evolving gender roles of the women's liberation era. The previous film versions had emphasized a behind-the-scenes look into Hollywood, the motion picture industry, and its pitfalls, but the reboot would set itself apart as a hard-edged musical bursting at the seams with sex, drugs, and rock and roll. The idea began with husband-and-wife writers John Gregory Dunne and Joan Didion, as a vehicle for James Taylor and Carly Simon, who were married at the time. Little did Dunne and Didion realize that their concept for a rock-musical remake of the 1954 Judy Garland film would become one of the most talked-about, controversial, and turbulent productions of the 1970s.

OPPOSITE: One-sheet poster from *A Star Is Born* (1976). Francesco Scavullo photographed the sexually provocative embrace of Barbra Streisand and Kris Kristofferson. This image became the cornerstone of the advertising and publicity campaigns for both the film and the soundtrack album.

Suggesting James Taylor and Carly Simon to star in a film together made perfect sense. At the time, Warner Bros. not only owned the remake rights for *A Star Is Born*, it also was affiliated with Warner Bros. Music Group, which had both artists under contract. When Dunne and Didion went to work on the screenplay, it was with Taylor and Simon in mind. The couple pitched their concept and the studio gave them a green light, declining to be incommoded by viewing the previous film versions or reading their scripts. Dunne remembered, "Warners wanted us to see the movie, but we assiduously refused to do it. We knew what it was about."[1] A front-page story in *Variety* formally announced the "third time around" remake, listing John Foreman as producer.[2] The screenwriters may not have watched the Judy Garland version, but their film's new working title had a very Garland ring to it: *Rainbow Road.*

The development of the project lost momentum until Barbra Streisand became involved at the urging of Jon Peters, an aspiring movie producer who was romantically involved with Streisand.

However, James Taylor and Carly Simon rejected the movie offer, citing that situations in the script hit a bit too close to home. When Hollywood talent agent Sue Mengers sent the screenplay to her biggest client, Barbra Streisand, Streisand also declined. At the time, the singer-actress was receiving some of the best notices of her career—as well as a Best Actress Oscar nomination—for her starring role in Sydney Pollack's *The Way We Were* (1973), opposite Robert Redford.

The development of the project lost momentum until Barbra Streisand became involved at the urging of Jon Peters, an aspiring movie producer who was romantically involved with Streisand. Peters had entered the entertainment business as a hairstylist to the rich and famous, with a chain of salons and a reputation as a charismatic ladies' man. Legend has it that Streisand noticed a woman at a party who was sporting a short shag haircut. Thinking that the look would be right for her latest film, Streisand asked the woman who had cut her hair, and the answer was "Jon Peters." Shortly thereafter, Streisand tracked down Peters and scheduled a meeting, much to his pleasure, as the hairstylist was smitten with Streisand. The two hit it off, and he designed the wig Streisand wore in the screwball comedy *For Pete's Sake* (1974).

Peters even served as record producer for Streisand's 1974 *ButterFly* album. Upon its release, most critics savaged the album because of its novice producer and its cliché cover art of a fly on a stick of butter. But as brutal as the press and critics were to Streisand and Peters on *ButterFly*, the reaction was nothing compared to the onslaught awaiting them on *A Star Is Born*.

During the production of Streisand's next movie, *Funny Lady* (1975), the sequel to *Funny Girl* (1968) (her film debut, that had earned her an Academy Award as Best Actress), Peters read the script for *Rainbow Road* and thought it was an ideal vehicle to contemporize Streisand's overall image, especially after playing an older character in a period film. Streisand recalled Peters telling her, "This is fantastic! You gotta make this movie, it'll be a big hit," to which she replied, "You know, it was made two times before." But he had no idea it was a remake, a fact that charmed Streisand. "He came to it purely, and what I started to think was this movie seems to work every twenty years. And I adored Judy Garland and Harold Arlen, these were two of my favorite people. Brilliant movie, brilliant performance by Judy, and an incredible score by Harold Arlen."[3]

With Streisand interested in the project, Warner Bros. faced a few major changes to the production. Their star agreed to appear in *Rainbow Road* only if the film was produced through her First Artists company and its soundtrack released on Columbia Records. She also wanted the title changed to *A Star Is Born*, a signal for audiences to expect a modern remake. Streisand said at the time, "I wanted to explore relationships *today*, as opposed to that of the 1930s and the 1950s."[4] Perhaps the most significant demand was Streisand's insistence that Jon Peters produce the film. Warner Bros. gave *A Star Is Born* a $6 million budget with any overages to be paid by Streisand. In lieu of payment for her services, the star would receive 25 percent of the

Frank Pierson and Barbra Streisand during production of *A Star Is Born* (1976). Tensions sometimes flared between the two during filming as the pair often disagreed on how a scene should be photographed.

gross profits and maintained final cut rights on the film. The studio, leaping at the chance to make a Barbra Streisand musical, agreed to all of her terms.

Streisand envisioned the film differently from its predecessors. The new version would be a radical departure from the dreamy Technicolor glamour of the 1937 drama, and the crowd-pleasing highs and lows of Judy Garland's 1954 musical *tour de force*. Streisand and Peters were dissatisfied with the Dunnes' script. They felt the love story lacked power and that the male lead role—a self-indulgent rock star named John Norman Howard (the middle name

Norman was a nod to the original story's protagonist)—was superior to the female, nightclub chanteuse Esther Hoffman. The Dunnes soon realized that what Peters and Streisand wanted was to put more of *their* love story on the screen, something that didn't sit well with them. After a year's work and three drafts of the screenplay, the Dunnes left the production, but not before making a deal with the studio for 10 percent of the gross for their labors.

With the departure of the Dunnes, the studio agreed that Jon Peters would produce and direct the film, with Streisand serving as executive producer. The industry scoffed at the idea of a neophyte director helming such an important production. The film's leading man posed another challenge. Kris Kristofferson had been connected with the project early on, and yet had refused to sign on officially. One of the reasons for his hesitation was that he wanted to be billed above the title with Streisand, a contract stipulation that Warner Bros. ironed out eventually. But before the studio finalized Kristofferson's involvement, it considered a slew of actor-singers for the role of John Norman Howard, including Marlon Brando (who had been courted for Garland's film version decades earlier), Neil Diamond, Mick Jagger, and Elvis Presley.

Streisand and Peters were still unhappy with the script. They approached *Dog Day Afternoon* (1975) screenwriter Frank Pierson for revisions. "Warner Bros. has asked me to 'do a fast rewrite'—is there ever a slow one?—of a rock-musical version of *A Star Is Born* and in a moment of mad ambition I accept on condition I can direct it as well. If it's okay with Barbra, it's okay with Warners—the decision is hers," Pierson wrote in 1976, prior the film's release.[5] Pierson was a seasoned professional, with two Academy Award nominations to his credit, for writing *Cat Ballou* (1965) and *Cool Hand Luke* (1967). However, Pierson's directing work up to that point mostly had been in television. He had only one theatrical feature film, *The Looking Glass War* (1970), to his name. Yet Streisand accepted the challenge, hiring Pierson both to write and direct. As for original story credit, that would be given to William A. Wellman and Robert Carson, who developed the first *A Star Is Born* incarnation for David O. Selznick back in 1937.

Pierson's screenplay revisions focused on further development of the Esther character, with considerable input from the actress who would portray her. As Streisand said at the time:

In the other film she just loved him. Well, I don't believe it. As you experience life, you also hate the person you love—and we deal with that in this movie. She doesn't stand around and watch him disintegrate through drink. She says, 'Fight for me, goddammit, protect yourself or I'll kill you!' I want to show in this movie what it's like to be a star—what the pressures are. The isolation. I wrote a lot of things into this movie that come from my own life. I will be revealed in this picture more than ever before. People watching will get to know Barbra Streisand a whole lot better.[6]

Further story updates revised the sexual stereotypes that audiences had become accustomed to in cinema: the man being the strong protector, who is physically and mentally superior to the woman, who passively stands behind her man. Updating Esther into a modern woman was essential for Streisand. Judy Garland's fiercely talented but passive 1950s heroine was out, and a new breed of woman was emerging. Streisand's Esther would be strong, independent, and indifferent to the role that society and the music business thought she should embody. "One of the things we've tried to do in this film is break down stereotypes, especially in relation to male and female role-playing," Streisand said. "We have a fight scene, and Kris cries. It's the *man* who cries. And we have a scene in a bathtub where I'm making him up as a woman."[7]

In early 1975, *A Star Is Born* was in preproduction and Rupert Holmes was engaged to write an all-original score. (He was also producing Streisand's 1975 album *Lazy Afternoon.*) After relocating to Los Angeles for the association, Holmes left the production on the basis of creative differences with the producer. Yet two of his compositions made it into the score: "Queen Bee" and "Everything." After Holmes's departure, Pierson suggested that songwriter Paul Williams write lyrics to Kenny Ascher's music. Williams, although brilliant, was an unpredictable collaborator. Still, the teaming of Williams and Ascher yielded five songs for the film. There were several other writers brought on to add additional tunes to round out the score, including Donna Weiss and pop-music mainstay Kenny Loggins, along with Alan and Marilyn Bergman.

The highlights of *A Star Is Born* (1976) are Streisand's "live" concert performances. Her powerful performance of the "With One More Look at You/Watch Closely Now" finale is truly electrifying.

Streisand herself was the catalyst behind what would become one of the most popular and recognized songs of her career. She had taken up studying the guitar with weekly lessons the previous year. It was while strumming the guitar that Streisand composed a melody that she played for Paul Williams during preproduction. Williams later recalled the first time he heard it: "The first thing she did, she said, 'Can you use this?' She picked up a guitar and played the melody. I said, 'Oh my God, it's beautiful.' She was like a little kid. It's a side of her I'd never seen before. She was like, 'You really like it?' I said, 'Like it? It's our love theme.' I wrote words to it."[8] "Evergreen (Love Theme from *A Star Is Born*)" became the breakout hit of the film and won the Academy Award for Music (Original Song).

With the majority of the music written, the studio hired Grammy Award–winning engineer and record producer Phil Ramone to step in and wrestle all the diverse compositions into a cohesive score. Streisand refused to lip-sync in the film. "I work in a very spontaneous way," she had said. "I work 'in the moment' and I can't lip-sync to something I recorded three months before."[9] She decided early in the production that all the singing in the film would be done live.

Warner Bros. cast Gary Busey as Bobby Ritchie, John Norman Howard's road manager. Busey, who had been acting in film and television for years, would get his breakout role in another rock-and-roll movie, playing the title role in *The Buddy Holly Story* (1978). In one of his appearances as an actor, director Paul Mazursky appears as Brian, John's friend and manager. The studio cast Streisand's friend and former supporting player in *The Way We Were*, Sally Kirkland, as the photographer, and Kristof-

Barbra Streisand performs for the thousands of concert "extras" at the Sun Devil Stadium in Tempe, Arizona, for *A Star Is Born* (1976). Not since her 1967 outdoor concert in Central Park had she appeared in front of such a large crowd.

ferson's then-wife, Rita Coolidge (along with singer Tony Orlando), played themselves in the Grammy Awards scene.

With three-time Oscar winner Robert Surtees as cinematographer and Peter Zinner as editor, the behind-the-scenes talent matched the star power seen on the screen. One behind-the-scenes credit caused some controversy after the film's release. In the end crawl, the credit "Miss Streisand's Clothes From...Her Closet" appeared, which caused a very unnecessary stir at the time. It received ridicule and, according to Streisand, she was "viciously attacked" for some of the costumes.[10] The press viewed the credit as Streisand's self-indulgence for wearing her personal wardrobe. She defended the costumes and her credit with a logical, creative reason, "I collect a lot of antique clothes and that's why it says in the credits, which was true, 'Miss Streisand's Clothes From...Her Closet' because they were things of mine, just antique things, a lot of antique things....We were also trying to save money, you have to remember. You know, I had to pay for anything over $6 million, right? Well, I didn't want to have a big costume budget."[11]

With the script, cast, and crew ready to go and with Streisand sporting a new, curly haircut, courtesy of Peters, filming on *A Star Is Born* commenced on February 2, 1976, at the Warner Bros. studios in Burbank (where the Garland film had been made) and nearby locations. From the first day of shooting, tensions flared between Streisand and Peters and director Pierson and, at times, between Streisand and Peters. Much like Sid Luft, Peters was inexperienced and in a bit over his head. Once word got out about discord on the set, the press became like vultures, exploiting, exaggerating, and even inventing negative pieces of gossip aimed at Streisand and the "hairdresser" producer.

Streisand's issues with Pierson were very personal, and her mistrust in him began on the very first day of filming. The night before, she and Pierson worked closely with Surtees on blocking the camera setups for the following day. When Streisand arrived on set in the morning, she discovered that Pierson had, without telling her, changed most of what they had

OPPOSITE: Missing from the previous incarnations of *A Star Is Born* was showing the immediate aftermath of the suicide of the male lead. For the first time on-screen, audiences were a witness to Esther's reaction to the tragedy. Streisand gives a very raw and emotional performance in the John Norman Howard (Kris Kristofferson) death scene.

agreed upon. This rattled and angered her. She and Pierson had agreed to be collaborators; feelings of betrayal began to grow. Thus began a struggle of creative control that would last until the film premiered in December. Streisand, always instinctive and creative, definitely had her opinions. As executive producer, she often clashed with Pierson's vision (or lack thereof) and began wielding her newfound power. "I never had the power before," Streisand said at the time. "If I did, some of my movies would have been better. When I record an album I have complete artistic freedom. But when I've made movies in the past, I haven't had the same freedom. The director would say one thing, and although I might disagree, I always gave in, you know, him being the director and all. And, of course, I had no say in the editing or anything like that. In this movie, I'm in control."[12] At one point during filming, getting angry at the constant tension between Streisand and Pierson, Kris Kristofferson exploded, "You two have to get your shit together! I don't care which of you wins, but this way, with two commanders, one sayin' retreat, the other advance…it's demoralizing the crew and puttin' me into catatonia!"[13]

The greatest logistical challenge facing the production was the huge outdoor concert set piece at Arizona State University's Sun Devil Stadium, in the city of Tempe. For a sense of authenticity on a grand scale, the studio recruited rock entrepreneur Bill Graham to produce, organize, and stage a mammoth rock concert for Pierson and his crew to shoot key scenes around. In a special Warner Bros. press release, Peters boasted, "Although this full day event is being arranged to draw crowds for the filming of our film, the musical end of it won't be just a few songs by each group, but a complete concert headlining Peter Frampton, Santana, Montrose, Graham Central Station, the L.A. Jets, and a lot of surprises. We're charging a nominal $3.50 admission to offset part of the cost of the day, but giving everybody attending an event worth two or three times that much."[14] An enthusiastic crowd of 47,000 extras cheered and reacted on cue and gave the film a key element of realism.

Upon completion of filming, the studio gave Pierson six weeks to finish his first cut of the film and then hold a screening of his version, with Streisand, Peters, and studio executives in attendance. After the screening, as Pierson recalled, "Barbra kisses me, and thanks me. It feels,

Jon Peters and Barbra Streisand arrive at the world premiere of *A Star Is Born* at the Village Theatre, Westwood, California, on December 18, 1976. The invitation asked that guests dress all in white or shades of gray. The new Hollywood "power couple" arrived dressed in black from head to toe.

somehow, like a good-bye kiss."[15] The following day, the production informed Pierson that Streisand was exercising her right of final cut and moving the editing to her Malibu home, where she has had installed all the required postproduction editing equipment. Streisand assembled a small crew of technicians who worked around the clock with her to finish the film before its world premiere on December 18, 1976, at the Village Theatre in Westwood, California.

Tensions and raw nerves were high the day of the opening. That night, klieg lights illuminated the sky over Westwood as reporters, photographers, and fans lined the streets and a long stream of limousines dropped off the Hollywood elites into the constant pop of flashbulbs. The invitations for the premiere announced "A Spectacular Night in White" and requested that all guests wear white or shades of gray. The crowd cheered as Streisand made her way into the theater wearing a *black* velvet dress and an antique cape with a tall fur collar. The amount of star power paled in comparison to the turnout for Garland's 1954 premiere, which was attended by over 250 stars. Along with costar Kristofferson (arriving in a white tuxedo), other celebrity guests on this night included Ryan O'Neal, Peter Bogdanovich, Helen Reddy, William Wyler, and George Cukor. Overall, the evening was a triumph for Streisand and Peters. Their film was a hit with the premiere audience and would soon become an even bigger smash with moviegoers across the country when it was released on Christmas Day.

Yet, the press greeted *A Star Is Born* largely with negative reviews. In the *Los Angeles Times*, Charles Champlin began his column lauding Streisand as "a distinctive personality, an expert comedienne, and an effective dramatic actress. Her voice is a glorious instrument…" He went on to write, "The disappointment—and it is—is that she and producer Jon Peters evidently chose not to share the creative responsibilities more widely. Too few cooks can spoil a broth,

Their film was a hit with the premiere audience and would soon become an even bigger smash with moviegoers across the country when it was released on Christmas Day.

too."[16] Vincent Canby in the *New York Times* was more specific, noting that Streisand "never plays to or with the other actors. She does *A Star Is Born* as a solo turn. Everyone else is a backup musician, which is okay when she's belting out a lyric, but distinctly odd when other actors come into the same frame."[17] Pauline Kael, writing for the *New Yorker*, remarked, "The picture has had the worst advance press I can recall (with the possible exceptions of *Cleopatra* and the 1954 *A Star Is Born*)." Kael described the songs as "often terribly slow and slurpy, with flight-of-fancy lyrics; they're disappointing throughout, with orchestrations that are fake gospel, fake soul, fake disco, or fake something else." She summed up her experience viewing the film observing, "Streisand has more talent than she knows what to do with, and the heart of a lion. But she's made a movie about the unassuming, unaffected person she wants us to think she is, and the image is so truthless she can't play it."[18]

Despite the poor reaction from the press, audiences across the country braved the frigid winter weather and flocked to see the film, making it one of the biggest moneymaking films of the year. With a domestic revenue of over $80 million, it became Streisand's most successful film to date. Audiences had a passionate connection to the film, a connection that went far beyond Streisand's loyal fan base. The film drew in a wide range of demographics; young and old alike took to the story and music. This, along with the international success of both the film and the soundtrack album, elevated Streisand to superstar status in the film industry. She was finally vindicated after the constant vitriol from the press.

The 1976 remake of *A Star Is Born* is, for the most part, a remake in name only. It has more disparities than similarities to Judy Garland's film. The basic premise is intact—a fading male star meets by happenstance a younger, up-and-coming, unknown female and helps make her a "star." Although still set in Los Angeles, the remake shifts its scenario from the glossy fantasy world of motion pictures during the era of the studio system to the sordid, volatile, drug-infused world of 1970s rock music. The world presented in the 1954 version is clean, bright, uncluttered and unthreatening. While the biggest crutch of Norman Maine was alcohol, John Norman Howard goes far beyond that with the inclusion of marijuana, cocaine, and sexual infidelities.

The character of Esther as embodied by Judy Garland is an innocent, somewhat naive young lady being thrust into a world that she is ill prepared to combat. Although demure, she possesses a power and an inner strength that grows as the story progresses. But this Esther also is a product of the 1950s and, as written, is a codependent who, despite being successful as a performer, feels herself a failure in her personal life because she can't "save" her man. While

there are moments when she is fully aware of her husband's self-destruction, like many women of the time, she feels powerless to rescue him as she doesn't have the wherewithal to help.

Streisand's Esther is a much more worldly woman, a product of the 1970s and women's liberation. She is a divorcée who finds contentment in herself and her aloneness and doesn't need a man to fulfill her emotionally or physically. She is a feminist, opinionated and with firm ideas. She knows where she's going and what she wants out of life. She wears men's suits several times in the film and she's the one who proposes marriage to John Norman Howard. Thus, she is far less vulnerable than previous Esthers. In his 2016 book-length critical essay, *Barbra Streisand: Redefining Beauty, Femininity, and Power*, Neal Gabler provides a succinct and perceptive overview of Streisand's film. Gabler views it less as a remake of *A Star Is Born* and more as a remake of Streisand's own *Funny Girl*, "…with the same Streisand conflations, only modernized to accommodate the new world of rock and roll, along with the new attitudes of feminism and the new attitudes toward romance of Streisand herself."[19]

The single release of "Evergreen (Love Theme from *A Star Is Born*)" and the full soundtrack album succeeded far beyond even Streisand's imagination. The album spent six weeks in the #1 position on Billboard's Top 200 LP chart, selling over 15 million copies worldwide. "Evergreen" went on to win Grammy awards as Song of the Year and Best Pop Vocal Performance, Female.

The awards season in 1977 brought many more accolades to Streisand's *A Star Is Born*. It won five Golden Globes, including Best Actress (Musical or Comedy) and Best Original Song. While Streisand was not nominated for an Oscar as Best Actress, the film did receive four Academy Award nominations: for Cinematography, Music (Original Song Score), Music (Original Song), and Sound. Streisand's Academy Award win for "Evergreen" was a personal triumph, and the making of her *Star Is Born* ultimately was the opposite of Garland's experience. Jon Peters went on to become a prolific film producer. Among his credits is producer of Bradley Cooper's *A Star Is Born* (2018).

OPPOSITE: The ultimate triumph for Barbra Streisand, pictured with Paul Williams, was winning the Academy Award for Best Original Song for composing the music for "Evergreen (Love Theme from *A Star Is Born*)" with lyrics by Williams.

Chapter Four

A STAR IS REBORN

MY MOTHER'S FUNERAL SERVICE WAS HELD IN NEW YORK CITY ON FRIDAY, June 27, 1969. A crowd of over 22,000 filed past her open casket to pay their respects to Judy Garland the performer, while those of us who knew her said a tearful good-bye to Judy the woman. Frank E. Campbell's Funeral Chapel had not experienced such an outpouring of public mourning since Rudolph Valentino's memorial back in 1926.

In the early morning of Saturday, June 28, a group of drag queens and their friends gathered at the Stonewall Inn, a gay bar in the West Village of Manhattan. Whether shock or grief had anything to do with it, these men and women spontaneously retaliated when a police raid—the latest among many—forced them into the street and closed the bar, where they had every right to be. They stood their ground against the astonished cops, who assumed the crowd would be agitated, but docile—sheep in women's clothing. But this final straw of police brutality had taken its toll. The crowd battled back. Stories vary, but the uprising carried on the next night, and the next. The rebellion was reported nationwide, the newspaper headlines and photographs documenting the conflict as a milestone for civil rights.

OPPOSITE: One-sheet poster for the 1983 reconstruction of *A Star Is Born* (1954), designed by illustrator Richard Amsel.

A portrait of me at the time of my debut at the London Palladium, 1976. A plaque and a photo of Mama from *A Star Is Born* are in the background. I feel Mama is always at my shoulder.

My mother's funeral and the Stonewall Uprising may be only circumstantially related, but the two events are often connected. As a remarkable moment in history that is linked to my family, we carry this connection with pride. (I was privileged to make my first visit to Stonewall in 2016 and am proud to be on the advisory committee of the nonprofit organization Stonewall Initiative Gives Back.) I know that my mother would have said that everybody at Stonewall did the right thing: They stood up for themselves. The gay community fought back against years of abuse just at the moment when they lost their legendary icon. My mother raised me to give back and not to simply take. If my mother was a spark in the Stonewall Uprising, then I want to be a part of that legacy as a tribute to her and the people who love her.

Since her death, the gay community has been instrumental in keeping my mother's star image, her movies, and her music, alive and thriving well into the twenty-first century. Her gay following was commented upon as early as the appearance of the Judy Garland cult, which dates back to the autumn of 1950 and began in earnest with her engagement at the Palace Theatre in New York in 1951. Around this time, a new awareness and admiration was blossoming for the adult Judy onstage; she was no longer the plucky teenager or the winsome young woman she had been on the screen. She had grown into the status of "living legend"—a distinction few performers ever achieve. Further, her persona was tinged with a new vulnerability and accessibility as a result of the recent headlines of her humiliating dismissal from MGM and her suicide attempt. In a period when gay men were, to put it mildly, repressed, many formed a strong attachment to Judy Garland.

Ten years later, at Carnegie Hall, Mama felt and acknowledged the intensity of her impact on audiences and the emotional connection that was established between her and the gay men who made up the better part of the crowd. I know because I was there and saw it for myself. My mother's way with a song, her intimate improvisations, called out to the "Friends of Dorothy," a triple-sided designation: a calling card, an endearment, or a slander. Judy Garland's most famous screen character—Dorothy of *The Wizard of Oz*—became slang for a gay man. It's no coincidence that the rainbow flag—a symbol of the lesbian, gay, bisexual, and transgender social movement—suggests "Over the Rainbow." Gays were attracted to Mama's

> My mother's way with a song, her intimate improvisations, called out to the "Friends of Dorothy," a triple-sided designation: a calling card, an endearment, or a slander.

rainbow of characteristics: her vibrancy, her humor, her insecurity, her vulnerability, and her self-consciousness. She played the asexual friend to Mickey Rooney in her early MGM days, as well as Dorothy Gale, the lonely and misunderstood young woman. Mama's most well-known songs exploit a certain lonesome solitude, expressing an inner longing: "Over the Rainbow" and "The Man That Got Away" are perfect examples. The former finds her yearning for a place happier and more colorful than the drab world she inhabits, the latter has her yearning for a love that can never be.

Especially in the film *A Star Is Born*, Mama was embraced by gay men and elevated to an integral part of their culture's iconography. Indeed, Mart Crowley's groundbreaking 1968 play *The Boys in the Band*, which became a famous gay film in 1970, drew its title from Norman Maine's line of encouragement to Esther before her screen test: "You're singing for yourself and the boys in the band." This phenomenon is even the subject of scholarly examination. In her 1992 essay "The Logic of Alternative Readings: *A Star Is Born*," Janet Staiger explores the relevant published material on the subject. Staiger considers how my mother's suffering, her theatricality, her instability, her intensity, her problems with her appearance, her choices in men, and her somewhat androgynous look in *A Star Is Born*, invite comparison between my mother and the men who elevated her as an early gay icon. The essay also examines how my mother's private life—rather than the life of the fictional character of Esther Blodgett/Vicki Lester—informs her gay fans' reaction to the movie.[1]

My mother—always forward-thinking—embraced her entire audience no matter what race, religion, or sexual orientation. She loved everyone. My mother even knew and loved Republicans, liberal as she was. When I appeared with my mother at that legendary last engagement at the Palace in 1967, the theater was always a sell-out and drew a diverse audience. Mama's gay fans were vocal and passionate, but they were not the overwhelming majority. Child fans were an important part of her story, too. They saw her on television in *The Wizard of Oz* and became instant admirers of the film and Judy Garland. This continues today. People come up to me all the time with their children and say how much they love Mama as Dorothy. My grandchildren call me "GG" and their great-grandmother "Triple G." My granddaughter, Jordan, told me in early autumn 2017, "I'm dressing as Triple G for Halloween!"

Mama soldiered on from crisis to crisis, often self-inflicted. The loyal "boys" couldn't save her, however, no matter how much love they held in reserve for her. She was over the rainbow before they knew it. Their loneliness and sense of otherness matched hers, from Dorothy Gale to Esther Blodgett to "the lady onstage," as Peter Allen affectionately wrote as a tribute to my mother many years after her death. Peter married my sister, Liza, in 1967, so he was my mother's son-in-law. (Liza and Peter divorced in 1974.) "Quiet please, there's a lady onstage," Peter sang. "She may not be the latest rage/But she's singing and she means it."

My mother's conviction to the lyric of a song was one of her great gifts. In a two-part autobiographical essay for *McCall's* magazine in 1964, my mother wrote:

> There's something about my voice that makes them see all the sadness and humor they've experienced. It makes them know that they aren't too different; they aren't apart. That's the only reason I can give for people's liking to hear me sing, because I'm not that fine a singer. Sometimes my vibrato is too fast or too slow, although I've got good pitch. I have good diction, and I read a song much more than I sing it.
>
> I try to bring the audience's own drama—tears and laughter they know about—to them. I try to match my lifelong experiences with theirs, and they match their own sadness and happiness to mine. I think that's it. Both men and women connect me with Dorothy in *The Wizard of Oz*, and they have a protective attitude toward me, which is rather sweet.[2]

One of the finest assessments of my mother's singing voice was provided by critic and author Henry Pleasants in his 1974 text *The Great American Popular Singers*. Pleasants describes her voice as follows:

> She had the most utterly *natural* vocal production of any singer I had ever heard. Probably because she sang so much as a child, and learned to appreciate the appeal of her child's voice, she made no effort as she grew older to produce her

> voice in any other way. It was an open-throated, almost birdlike vocal production, clear, pure, resonant, innocent. One keeps coming back to that word *innocent*, again and again. It was not just an innocent sound. More importantly, it was a sound innocent of anything that smacked of artful management.[3]

Though just a young girl, my mother had the capability to tap into the emotional content of words wrapped in a melody. The Judy Garland of Kansas and Oz, at sixteen, turned an "I wish" song into a meditation on loneliness and longing. Before *The Wizard of Oz*, Mama was star-struck, in love from afar in "You Made Me Love You." After it, she pined for "The Boy Next Door" in *Meet Me in St. Louis*. She headed out West "On the Atchison, Topeka and the Santa Fe," in *The Harvey Girls*, and took the stage to "Be a Clown" for *The Pirate*. In *Summer Stock*, she urged everyone to "Get Happy" with a conviction that implied she was trying to convince herself as well. And then, suddenly, she was older and wiser, thanks to having her heart broken by "The Man That Got Away." Her life and personality can be found in her music. She was, by her own admission, most alive and her true self when she was singing. This personal truth even made it into *A Star Is Born*: "I somehow feel most alive when I'm singing," Esther Blodgett tells Norman Maine early in their relationship. As Roger Edens composed in his lyric of special material for my mother's first appearance at the Palace Theatre, and reworked for the "Born in the Trunk" sequence of *A Star Is Born*, "The history of my life is in my songs."

As the longing in her voice indicates, Mama was a searcher. She was always looking—looking for the right time to be a mother, for the right audience to appreciate how much she had to share, for the right man to be her partner in whatever came next, and for the right place to call home. She was still searching when she died.

Beyond the initial New York City television broadcast in 1961, my mother refused to watch *A Star Is Born* after the 1954 premieres in Los Angeles, New York City, and Chicago. Once the film had been butchered, it was difficult for her to sit and relive the making of this scene or that, that number or this, knowing what had been on the screen and could never be again, knowing what so many viewers had missed. It was too painful for her. George Cukor felt the same way. In a letter to production designer Gene Allen in 1979, Cukor revealed that he refused to see the shortened version. Although he had never seen it, he was aware of all the cuts and what scenes were lost. He wrote Allen that the film's final edit was "Jack Warner's last crime! I've been used to cuts in pictures that I've done but this one strikes me as irreparable and tragic. Maybe tragic is too pompous a word—but it was awfully sad and unnecessary."[4]

I agree. It was sad, and I thought, as Mr. Cukor said, "irreparable." There was nothing to be done, too much time had passed. I had to let it go. When I first saw the film, I remember my favorite scene—very short, but sweet. Within the movie-studio gates, the Southern California sun shines brightly. Esther, in a cute little dress and perky hat, gets in line at the payroll booth, at the "*A* through *K*" window, but is told to go the next one, where she repeats her name, "Blodgett." The clerk finds her under *L*, then spells out the name: "V-i-c-k-i L-e-s-t-e-r." Esther is at first perplexed, then thoughtful, then resigned, then pleased, speaking the name aloud, as she walks away with her paycheck. My mother, I think, did that many times, both inside and outside the studio gates. Blindsided by circumstance, she would gather herself and move on.

I was very touched by the ending of *A Star Is Born*, but I was struck by how strange it was that Esther didn't sing. This was a musical disguised as a drama, with no grand finale. I was entranced by the scene in the little motel room, where Esther sings, partly a cappella, to Norman Maine, "It's a New World." It's a lovely ballad, tender and optimistic. It's my favorite song in the film.

The movie also left me pondering very personal questions. I was startled by the scenes in which Esther/Vicki desperately attempts to care for and save her addict husband. The sequence in the dressing room, where she's dressed in the costume of a freckled, ragamuffin newsboy, was devastating to me. Esther is confiding to her friend (and Norman's), the head of the studio, and holding back tears, venting her frustration and desperation. Explaining how much she loves him, yet sometimes hates him for failing. Then she goes on, "But…I hate me, too." She feels a sense of shame for failing, for not being enough for the man she loves. Esther breaks down in an emotional spiral that was very familiar to me. I had been a similar caregiver for my mother in her later years. I knew exactly what had driven Esther to tears.

After watching *A Star Is Born* for the first time, I immediately called my father in Los Angeles to inquire about this particular scene. "Did she know what she was saying?" I asked. "Did she know she was talking about herself?" Without a pause, he responded, "You bet she did. That's why it's so good." I realized at that moment that in real life, my mother was Esther Blodgett and Vicki Lester, but there were traits in her—especially her drug dependency—that strongly echoed the character of Norman Maine.

My father agreed with me. My mother was an unpredictable woman. He came to know her after her MGM contract was cancelled and the subject of Hollywood gossip, rumors, and blind items published in the magazines and newspapers. After they met, my mother and father worked together to put the star back on her feet for some very successful concerts. These events raised her profile once again, sparked new interest in Judy Garland, and paved the way for a comeback in movies. It didn't get past Dad that there was a twist here. The comeback, *A Star Is Born*, was filled with overtones—dark and light—that echoed my mother's life.

My father knew the great risk they were both taking, but had confidence that his new wife could pull it off—even under the spell of drugs and alcohol. Dad admitted to ignoring the bottom line, the movie, as everyone in town knew. He allowed it to go way over budget. Then after premiering, the re-cut movie failed, and my mother failed, too, sending her careening into a downward spiral of depression and deeper drug dependency. My dad always said, "I know that I did the best I could do, and it still wasn't enough."[5]

As my mother's sometimes-caregiver, I had experienced her at her worst. The Nembutal, the Seconal, and the Tuinal were supplemented at some point with Ritalin. She was taking fifty to one hundred milligrams per day—more than double the normal dose. With no turnaround in sight, she kept forging ahead, digging deeper ruts as she spun her wheels. At that time, there were only a few sanitariums and clinics for treatment, the kind Norman Maine is subjected to in the film. There was no Betty Ford Center, no comfortable private retreats. So, the story of *A Star Is Born* was a very personal, and unfortunately biographical, tale.

Once I saw the parallels between the movie and Mama's life, I began to wonder: was there more to learn in the rumored missing pieces of the puzzle? The precise storytelling that I was used to seeing in a Hollywood movie was absent in the first half. It was confusing and disorienting. What happened between Esther's trancelike walk up the stairs after informing Danny of her decision and the big jump to the makeup room at the studio? Where did the plot go, the logic, the motivations? Where was the love story? I was so close to the heart of the matter, I wondered if anyone else cared about this movie the way I did.

A Star Is Born was kept alive in a butchered form as late-night television programming and remembered fondly by those lucky few who had seen and remembered the film in its original full-length version.

I've always been clearheaded about the great highs and shattering lows that being Judy Garland's daughter has brought with it. The responsibility I feel to my mother's legacy is to always ensure that her talent and image are held in high regard, with respect, and with honor— for her work and what she gave as an actress, a singer, and an entertainer. One of the most extraordinary comebacks my mother ever made happened after her death. *A Star Is Born* was kept alive in a butchered form as late-night television programming and remembered fondly by those lucky few who had seen and remembered the film in its original full-length version. It was also revered by Judy Garland fans. By the 1970s, Mama's *A Star Is Born* had become a cult classic rather than a great film.

Near the top of my list of things I wanted in life was to see *A Star Is Born* as my parents and George Cukor had crafted it and intended it to be seen. All the "shoulds" apply here. It should have been seen in its full 181-minute glory in its initial general release. It should not have been so harshly cut, and the resulting remnants scattered so carelessly. It should have been the high point of Act II of Judy Garland's career, not the vast disappointment that shadowed Act III. I (and many others) also felt it should have been nominated for Best Picture. It should have won Mama the Best Actress Oscar, and, along with it, Hollywood's approval. The movie should have confirmed in everyone's eyes that, when my mother was good, she was the very best. Finally, in 1983, my wish came true: *A Star Is Born* was transformed and reborn into a treasured happy ending for me.

In the late 1970s and early 1980s, there was an evolving atmosphere of concern for the state of Hollywood classics. Cable television and the advent of home video began generating a greater interest in older films. Those who cared about film history were appalled to discover that old negatives and prints of some of the greatest films were often missing, uncatalogued, or sitting deteriorating in studio vaults and rented warehouses. Ronald Haver, at the time head of the Film Department at the Los Angeles County Museum of Art (LACMA), thought he might have a chance to rescue one of his favorite films, *A Star Is Born* from 1954. He thought maybe he could restore the film that everyone knew was incomplete—"a vandalized masterpiece," as Christopher Finch aptly described it in his 1975 critical biography *Rainbow: The Stormy Life of Judy Garland*.[6] Haver suspected the 181-minute premiere version might be out there somewhere. This was a film preservationist's golden opportunity to combine the love of his job with the love of this movie he had first seen when he was sixteen years old.

In 1974, Haver had already curated a George Cukor retrospective at LACMA. The director had declined his invitation to attend the screening of *A Star Is Born*. In October 1981, Haver was involved with a tribute evening to Ira Gershwin at the Academy of Motion Picture Arts and Sciences, the highlight being my mother's superb interpretation of "The Man That Got

OPPOSITE: A photo depicting the editing of *A Star Is Born*. Film editor Folmar Blangsted is examining a strip of 35mm film while leaning on a Moviola. (The image on the screen is a still photograph of Norman Maine and Vicki Lester planning their Malibu beach home.)

Away" in an original 35mm four-track stereo print on Eastmancolor film stock. Also included was her audio recording of Gershwin and Harold Arlen's jingle for the Trinidad Coconut Oil Shampoo commercial, unearthed by the singer and music revivalist Michael Feinstein (who at that time was working as the archivist of Ira Gershwin). This audio was from one of the scenes that had been cut and discarded. Although the sound quality was poor and missing the visual component, the discovery was significant, and led to further interest in the film's restoration.

Another catalyst to the project was the success of Barbra Streisand's 1976 version; if Streisand's interpretation could find such an enormous audience, then perhaps the time was right to revive Judy Garland's. My friends knew I wanted to see the original cut of the film. Film critic Rex Reed was in touch with a man who claimed to have an uncut print of *A Star Is Born* from an uncle who had been a projectionist and refused to cut the film back in 1954. However, he was reluctant to show us the print for fear that it might be confiscated by Warner Bros. or even the FBI for theft of a film print he had no right to own. He kept making us communicate with him at various pay telephone booths in New York City until we convinced him we weren't working with the authorities but simply wanted to see the uncut version of *A Star Is Born*. Rex arranged a screening room and we ordered champagne and caviar in celebration. We looked at the stack of film canisters that read *A Star Is Born* and my nerves were on edge. I was cautious, but consumed by curiosity and excitement. We sat back in our chairs and dimmed the lights and on came a black-and-white copy of the MGM musical *Good News* (1947), with "The French Lesson" number cut out. Kay Thompson, who was in the screening room, remarked, "Well, taken once again!" The film appeared cursed. So much for that caper.

Ron Haver was more fortunate. Academy president Fay Kanin and Gene Allen were enthusiastic about the idea of attempting to restore the original cut of the film. Allen contacted George Cukor, whose response was, "Very intriguing, by all means—go ahead with it."[7] The Academy then formally approached Robert Daly, chairman of Warner Bros., for the necessary permission and to finance Haver's search. The assent was given, and Haver began to examine the Warner Bros. paper files and film storage on both East and West Coasts.

The proposal scene of Norman and Vicki on the soundstage. This was cut after the premiere. Photo by Sanford Roth.

Dave Strohmaier, an apprentice editor at Warner Bros., located the complete 181-minute monaural soundtrack in the studio sound library, but, unfortunately, not all of the camera footage to accompany it. Searches at the Technicolor laboratory, rummages at various film exchanges, and inquiries to private collectors consumed months of Haver's time. In an unmarked can, Haver did find one complete scene—the proposal with Vicki Lester singing "Here's What I'm Here For" and the microphone pickup of Norman and Vicki's intimate conversation. At the studio stock footage library, Haver discovered fragments of outtakes from scenes included in the full-length version. Best of all, he located an alternate take of "Lose That Long Face." Although he had the complete 181-minute soundtrack, and had found two cut musical numbers, over twenty minutes of camera footage remained missing. Haver decided to build a reconstruction of the film with a mint condition Technicolor negative of the shorter

ABOVE: Mama as a carhop in a scene deleted after the film's premiere. Actor Chick Chandler is behind the wheel.
OPPOSITE, FROM TOP: Mama dressed as a carhop with director George Cukor on location at Robert's Drive-In, Hollywood. • My mother and father during production of the carhop sequence.

Mama flanked by child actors Patricia Rosamond and Bobby Sailes in the "Lose That Long Face" musical number. The entire number was cut shortly after the film's premiere in 1954 and the footage remained lost for nearly thirty years. Photo by Bob Willoughby

version as his main image source, the 154 minutes of stereo soundtrack on the studio's reference print, and the 181 minutes of monaural soundtrack as the basis for his work. Haver thought that by using the footage he had located, supplemented by still photographs from the film, he could create animated photo montages paired with the surviving soundtrack.

Once it was discovered that twenty minutes of the picture were permanently lost, the studio suggested a demonstration of how the still photos might be layered over the surviving soundtrack before investing $30,000 for the full reconstruction. Once a sample of Haver's reconstruction work was ready, a private screening was arranged at the Academy for Robert Daly. George Cukor was invited as well and accepted the invitation. Sadly, he died of heart failure two days before the screening, on January 24, 1983, at the age of eighty-three. Nevertheless, the screening went on and everyone was pleased with the results. Cukor's sudden death galvanized everyone into action: the film must be completed as a tribute to the late director and as a case study in the importance of preservation. The reconstruction was filled with high drama. For example, D. J. Ziegler of the Academy Film Department worked long hours on "Lose That Long Face," in order to synchronize the sound to the silent outtake footage. After the reconstruction was completed and first shown, the original negative of "Lose That Long Face" surfaced among 1,200 film reels seized by the Los Angeles district attorney's office from a Burbank storage facility. A private collector had spirited the reels of film away from the Warner Bros. studios. It was eventually inserted into Haver's reconstruction. Although Cukor had died, Gene Allen served as advisor on the look and feel of the lost sequences when they were re-created using still photographs.

And that's how *A Star Is Born* was reborn. Hollywood is a town of second acts, and my mother had more comebacks than anyone. Now, with most of its original footage restored, Mama's big movie was positioned to make a stunning comeback of its own.

In the meantime, the Academy was preparing a publicity campaign for the announcement of the restoration, to be followed by the fanfare for a "world re-premiere" at Radio City Music Hall in New York City. A vintage movie like *A Star Is Born* would not ordinarily be given the big-screen theatrical treatment outside of museums, archives, and revival theaters; however, Abel Gance's silent masterpiece, *Napoléon* (1927), had set an important precedent two years earlier. The film had been reconstructed with a new musical score composed and conducted by Carmine Coppola (father of Francis Ford Coppola), and the movie was given its American premiere at Radio City Music Hall in 1981, where it sold out the 6,000-seat theater during its run. The Academy felt *A Star Is Born* should be afforded the prestige of *Napoléon*, and believed they could fill the 6,000-seat theater for one night.

The film would then travel to Washington, D.C.; Oakland, California (Oakland was selected, rather than San Francisco, because it could offer the art-deco glamour and the size of the Paramount Theatre); Beverly Hills (at the Academy's Samuel Goldwyn Theater); Chicago;

CLOCKWISE FROM TOP LEFT: Esther washes her hair on the roof of the rooming house. • Esther calls out to Norman from the roof of the rooming house. • Esther waits by the Oleander Arms swimming pool for a telephone call from Norman Maine that never comes. OPPOSITE: Esther in the rooming house.

and Dallas. A co-sponsor, with the Academy, would host the event in each city: in New York City, the Museum of Modern Art; in Washington, the American Film Institute; in Oakland, the Pacific Film Archive; in Beverly Hills, Warner Bros., Inc.; in Chicago, the Chicago International Film Festival; and the co-sponsor in Dallas would be the USA Film Festival. All proceeds would go to film preservation projects at each institution.

Richard Amsel, the gifted graphic designer, was selected by Warner Bros. to create a new poster for the restored film. He chose the arresting, touching, and lovely image of my mother's hands framing her face in the number "Someone at Last" when she imagines her "big, fat close-up." (The still photograph from this scene had, by this time, become an iconic Garland image.) Amsel heightened and brightened its coloration, changed the costume from the oversized man's pink dress shirt to the navy-blue dress from "The Man That Got Away," and added silvered searchlights to back it all up against a starry Hollywood night sky. He made the familiar image more sophisticated, more contemporary, and sexier.

The finishing touches to sight and sound were wrapped up while Gene Allen worked with the tinting of the still photographs that would be used to fill in the gaps of missing footage. It was decided that an intermission would immediately follow "Born in a Trunk," to give the audience a break as the running time was extended. With this, Haver and his team were virtually done. Tickets to attend the film at Radio City Music Hall ranged in price. Haver and a young editor named Craig Holt put together a special preview premium—with a fifty-dollar admission—to attend a cocktail reception prior to the film in the lounge of Radio City Music Hall. After the film and the evening's speeches, the audience was given a rare treat: old newsreel footage of the 1950s glam-fest that was the original Pantages premiere in Hollywood.

A throng of fans and press, along with a long line of limousines, greeted my sister, Liza, and me as we passed under the marquee that read, "The Academy Foundation Presents *A Star Is Born*." Our mother's costar, James Mason, joined us, and special guest Lillian Gish arrived. Also in attendance were Helen Hayes, Andy Warhol, Candice Bergen, Patricia Neal, and many other supportive faces. I'm told that it was the most exciting night in Ron Haver's life. In *New York* magazine, film critic David Denby described the evening as "the most stirring event of the summer movie season foundering in mediocrity," and noted the electric atmosphere created by "6,000 adults concentrating on a thirty-year-old film that meant something to them emotionally."[8]

Academy president Fay Kanin was eloquent in her introduction: "All art forms are buffeted by time, but ours has proved unexpectedly ephemeral. Museums can show us sculpture from fifteen hundred years ago and beautifully preserved books and paintings....But most of the movies made before 1920 have already been lost to us....The nation's film archives have done a heroic job...but they need help and they need it soon."[9] I was proud to be a small part of this groundbreaking moment for the burgeoning movement of film preservation.

I shared a few thoughts as well, confiding to thousands, "All my life I've wanted to see this movie the way my mother and father made it."[10] My dream came true that night. The thundering applause started early in the evening. The audience truly appreciated the plot-holes that were finally filled, and the music that was lost, now restored. The clapping and cheering

"Hello, everybody. This is Mrs. Norman Maine."

seemed to continue without a pause for more than two minutes after my mother, as Esther Blodgett, stepped out onto an enormous stage into the spotlight and carefully began, "Hello, everybody," then continued proudly, "This is Mrs. Norman Maine."

My father was in attendance that night as well. One memory I will treasure always is how Liza and I held each other close and cried for nearly twenty minutes in a dressing room back-stage after the screening. For both of us, Mama was right there on the big screen just as we remembered her in life, and her masterpiece had finally been restored to its full glory. It was such a cathartic experience for my family. The entire evening was a blur of excitement, relief, and tears. How could such a great movie have been so poorly handled? My father, in his later years, gave this explanation, "We did too much of everything. Too much movie and too much music. It was good too much."[11]

The inclusion of still photograph montages in the reconstruction was controversial. To this day, the sudden switch to sepia-toned images is accused by some of confusing or jolting viewers out of the movie as it strives to convey the missing film footage to synchronize with the complete soundtrack. Critic Janet Maslin, writing for the *New York Times* in 1983, noted that the nine scenes that combine dialogue, stock footage, and still photographs "…bring the film to a temporary halt. The still photographs, in particular, have a candid and almost melancholy feeling, in contrast to the more glamorous material that surrounds them. It's a measure of the film's enormous seductiveness that these interruptions seem so startling. A movie that cast less of a spell could tolerate this kind of intrusion far more easily."[12]

A Star Is Born's reconstruction became a template for film restoration of this kind. The Museum of Modern Art's two major D. W. Griffith restorations, *Way Down East* (1920) and *Intolerance* (1916), restored in 1984 and 1989, respectively, used photographs and frame enlargements to bridge missing sequences, as did the reconstruction of Frank Capra's *Lost Horizon* (1937) in 1986. Haver wrote about his mission to reconstruct the film, first in *American Film* magazine in an article called "*A Star Is Born* Again: The Classic Restored" in the July/August 1983 issue, creating interest in the film and his methods. Several years later, he expanded upon his article and wrote a book, *A Star Is Born: The Making of the 1954 Movie and Its 1983 Restoration*, published in 1988.

I had finally met Ron Haver, the tireless detective behind the reconstruction, the night before the big premiere, at a press reception at Quo Vadis restaurant. I was there, escorted by my father. Kitty Carlisle Hart, widow of Moss Hart, was there, too. After the New York City screening, my family attended the first of the four public screenings at the Academy's Samuel Goldwyn Theater in Beverly Hills, held on July 19, 1983. The opening night was a star-filled event. Lillian Gish graced the occasion, as did Gregory Peck. To my delight and thrill, so many who worked on the film attended and showed their support, including Gene Allen, Sam Leavitt, and Lucy Marlow.

James Mason attended the screening, as well as a champagne reception beforehand. I remember him being asked about *A Star Is Born* that night. He considered Norman Maine among his greatest performances. When asked if he might have won an Oscar in 1955 had Academy members seen the full-length version, he replied, "I think so, yes." Mason was enjoying himself, but my father was having an uneasy time of it, feeling his prominent role in the original production had been minimized. He felt invisible at these events. But with the eventual sales to television and home video came some sense of satisfaction that the film was no longer a financial failure. According to him, "The film would earn back every penny, plus an ongoing profit."[13] Galvanized by the success of *A Star Is Born*, my father licensed footage from *The Judy Garland Show* and television special clips to make possible *Judy Garland: The Concert Years*, a ninety-minute documentary first broadcast on PBS in 1985.

I was overjoyed at the positive reception *A Star Is Born* received, and felt ready to reveal more about my mother. I had never really shared my memories publicly, with the exception of Gerold Frank's exhaustive 1975 biography of my mother, *Judy*. My entire family cooperated with that book. However, years later, when I decided to write an autobiography, *Me and My Shadows: A Family Memoir*, published in 1998, my father resented that I wanted to tell my story. I was of the opinion that this was *my* story. If my father, Liza, or Joe wanted to write *their* story, that was fine by me and they would have my full support. My father, however, did not see it that way. "Don't fuck with my property," he told me, and threatened to sue me. It was clear to me that envy was at the root of his anger. He had hoped to write a book, too, but was unable or unwilling to see it through to completion (My father's autobiography, begun in the 1960s and left unfinished at the time of his death, was published in 2017.) The fireworks that ensued between us were like the Fourth of July. There was no litigation or any literary work forthcoming from my father; he was simply angry that I had done what he had wanted and failed to do.

Adding fuel to the fire was the adaptation of *Me and My Shadows* into a major network event, telecast by ABC across two consecutive nights: *Life with Judy Garland: Me and My Shadows* (2001), starring Judy Davis. When that film won five Emmy Awards, the jealousy nearly choked my father. Sadly, he always blamed his failures on anyone and everyone else, rather than holding himself accountable. We didn't speak to each other for several years. We did make tentative amends before he died, but there was still a rift between us. We left messages on each other's answering machines, but did not see each other in person. I tried to love whatever was left of him that hadn't been strangled by his overwhelming sense of lost opportunity. My father died on September 15, 2005, in Los Angeles, at the age of eighty-nine. My brother Joe lived with him and served as his primary caregiver in his last years.

I've forgiven my father long ago. I've forgiven his bitterness in blaming Hollywood—which possessed him—instead of looking at himself and realizing he couldn't save Mama or rescue the film. When you point a finger at someone, you have three fingers pointing back at yourself. *A Star Is Born* haunted him and was a desperately painful memory for him. He had seen the hard work and the perfect final product. To have that vision cut and to slash away my mother's great film career and excise my father's desire to prove himself as a producer sent him on a journey of always blaming someone else. I excuse my father's behavior as I know how much he loved Mama. His brash bravado, his lovable and charming personality, turned to sour victimization, like Norman Maine with his career. It's very sad for me.

I had not seen *A Star Is Born* theatrically—on a big screen with a large, appreciative audience—since the time of the 1983 reconstruction when I was thirty years old. The film changed for me once again when I saw it at the Turner Classic Movies Classic Film Festival on April 22, 2010. This was the network's first event of this kind, and they chose Judy Garland and *A Star Is Born* to be the opening night gala presentation at the Chinese Theatre on Hollywood Boulevard, several blocks away from the site of the original premiere. The movie had been buffed and shined with digital sound, new color corrections, and a critical reputation as a classic film that dated back twenty-seven years. I was now a mature adult, and the movie had been restored once more to such a degree that I watched it with new eyes. Better still, I was able to take my two children.

I was thrilled to share with my son, Jesse, and my daughter, Vanessa, the world premiere of the new digital version of my mother's musical masterpiece. Thanks to digital technology, the ravages of time were removed

With my children Vanessa Jade Richards and Jesse Cole Richards at the opening-night gala premiere of a newly restored edition of *A Star Is Born* at the first Turner Classic Movies Film Festival, April 2010. Photo by WENN Ltd./Alamy Photo.

from the film and the 1983 reconstruction efforts to reinstate the cuts made shortly after the film's 1954 premiere were further remedied. It was quite an event for us all.

For many years, *A Star Is Born* was an upsetting experience for me. The film's story, and its underlying message about fame and addiction, hit too close to home. The massive disappointment of the film at the time hardened my mother's heart about Hollywood. The enthusiastic reaction of my children spurred me to open up the photographs and memories about the film

I have carefully kept and privately collected for decades. Now I could watch and discuss the film with a more optimistic outlook. Mama's movie had not only been restored to its orignial glory, but had touched and brought joy to so many people. In a way, the accolades the film was receiving decades later helped to soothe the pain it had caused me in the past.

A Star Is Born is the quintessential Hollywood story of a young star on the rise, and her star-lover-mentor destroying himself. While she is on the way up, he is on the way down. All the while, the cruel seesaw of the Hollywood machine is driving them both. Looking back, I see *A Star Is Born* as the glorious high of the latter part of my mother's career. It also marked a bitter low point, and signaled the beginning of the end. Esther and Norman's extreme high-and-low story was a poignantly fitting parable of my mother's life and an ideal star vehicle for her persona. But its failure also hurt her deeply and showed her that Hollywood held a grudge, that her hoped-for cinematic comeback was not meant to be. It was a deeply personal project for her, and I now feel the same way about the movie. Like me and my brother Joe, *A Star Is Born* was a product of Judy Garland and Sid Luft. It is part of our family. It is the most touching, exhilarating, and unforgettable home movie imaginable, and I'm so glad it exists. After I was first diagnosed with breast cancer in 2013, I was on my way to my first appointment with Dr. David Agus to discuss a treatment strategy. I was terrified and scared out of my wits. On the way, I stopped at the Lazy Daisy, a hippy-dippy café on Wilshire Boulevard in Beverly Hills. I looked up and, behind the coffee cans, saw they had a 1983 Richard Amsel-designed poster from *A Star Is Born* behind the counter. I saw that as a sign that Mama and Dad were on my shoulders, looking over me. I knew then I was going to be all right.

A Star Is Born is not just a film. It's a vision of a whole world, an accurate depiction of how Hollywood as an institution functions. Despite ostensibly being a musical, the emphasis is not on music. The film is as concerned with genuine emotions as it is with incorporating song and dance. The plot is the centerpiece of the film and the songs illustrate the plot. It is a complete reversal of the typical film musical up to that time. Before then, many musicals were light comedies with a plot loosely strung together by songs, the "backstage musical" was popular in the 1930s, but Mama was weary of lightweight plots by the time of *Summer Stock* and wanted something different for her future film work.

The Wizard of Oz and *A Star Is Born* are arguably my mother's two greatest films. *The Wizard of Oz* is exceptional—a film that beautifully conveys the wonders, as well as the anxieties, of childhood. It is a perfect film musical with an impeccable score highlighted by "Over the Rainbow," which always will be associated with my mother. Like Dorothy in *The Wizard of Oz*, Esther Blodgett/Vicki Lester in *A Star Is Born* is earnest, innocent, and appealing, yet displays a strong inner quality that allows her to persevere.

Today, my mother's film is readily available for anyone who wishes to see it in a version as close to the original version as possible.

Tributes to my mother in *A Star Is Born* are not hard to come by these days, but I was especially touched by the praise given to her and her favorite film by colleagues over forty years after her death. Mickey Rooney, who starred or appeared in ten of my mother's films, maintained, "Judy gave the finest performance of her career in *A Star Is Born*. It was the perfect showcase for all her God-given talent."[14] Margaret O'Brien, who played her younger sister, Tootie, in *Meet Me in St. Louis*, observed, "*A Star Is Born* is one of the greatest performances ever captured by the movies. Judy did everything in *A Star Is Born*. She sang, and she danced, she did comedy, and she gave a magnificent dramatic performance."[15] Angela Lansbury, who costarred as Em, the dancehall girl, in *The Harvey Girls*, as well as appearing in *Till the Clouds Roll By* (both 1946) offered, "Judy was an extraordinary talent who made several classic movies, but—as a performance—*A Star Is Born* is her masterpiece."[16] Finally, Lauren Bacall volunteered, "*A Star Is Born* is Judy's greatest performance....I still haven't forgiven the Academy for not honoring her brilliant work in that movie."[17] John Fricke summed up the prevailing view in his 2011 illustrated filmography, *Judy: A Legendary Film Career*. "*A Star Is Born* somehow withstood all its excesses, pro and con, to acquire and maintain instant stature as Judy Garland's preeminent motion picture performance."[18]

Two months after the TCM Classic Film Festival presentation, on the forty-first anniversary of my mother's passing, the newly digitized version was released to home video, where it remains available as a DCP (Digital Cinema Package) to be shown theatrically, on home video, for downloading, and streaming. Today, my mother's film is readily available for anyone who wishes to see it in a version as close to the original version as possible. What could be more rewarding for me and for every fan of the movie?

The following year, it was reported that Clint Eastwood, Bill Gerber, and Jon Peters were in the midst of planning a new version, to star Beyoncé Knowles, with Eastwood directing. Later, it was reported that Beyoncé withdrew from the project. In 2015, it was publicized that Bradley Cooper was to make his directorial debut with a new take on *A Star Is Born*. Lady Gaga and Cooper were to play the leading roles and production commenced in 2017 with significant footage shot at the Coachella Festival and featuring songs written for the film by Gaga, Cooper, and a handful of artists. Cooper plays seasoned musician Jackson Maine, while Lady Gaga portrays Ally, a struggling artist, with Andrew Dice Clay, Dave Chappelle, and Sam Elliot among the supporting cast. Another announcement came in 2017: Bill Condon was signed to develop a Broadway musical version of *A Star Is Born* based on the 1954 screenplay and music. I look forward to seeing the result of these efforts, and wish these talented artists all the best as they travel the illustrious road of *A Star Is Born*.

ONE LINGERING OBLIGATION I HAD TOWARD MY MOTHER INVOLVES HER final resting place. I was only sixteen when she died. Rather than her own children, Mickey Deans, as widower, had the legal authority to make all the decisions. Liza was consulted, but Joe and I were not, and ultimately Deans decided that my mother should be buried at Ferncliff Cemetery in Hartsdale, New York, about twenty-five miles north of Manhattan. Over a year after she died (at Liza's expense) she was interred in the Ferncliff Mausoleum, unit 9, alcove HH, crypt 31, on November 4, 1970, in a beige polished marble vault carved with the inscription, "JUDY GARLAND 1922–1969." I never went to the cemetery, as it didn't mean anything to me. I had no emotional attachment to the location and neither did my mother. I remember Peter Allen encouraging me to believe that Ferncliff wasn't where she really was anyway, and to think of her as always being with me. Nevertheless, the way it was handled always bothered me. But as long as Mickey Deans was alive, I had no recourse. When Mickey died in Cleveland, Ohio in 2003, my family was empowered to make a change. We felt that Hollywood Forever Cemetery should be the final resting place for Mama, so as next of kin I took it upon myself to spearhead the moving of my mother to Hollywood. As Liza, Joe, and I all live in Southern California, the location made sense to everyone. We all agreed and officially signed off on it. With the help of Tyler Cassidy at Hollywood Forever, as well as Michael Feinstein, who was an enormous help with the legal and logistical issues involved, we brought Mama home to Hollywood.

I worked on the colors of the stone and the inscription. I put a great deal of thought into what my mother would have loved—as opposed to what me or my sister or my brother would want. This was her place. I selected a rose-colored marble with her name in a chocolate brown color: "JUDY GARLAND JUNE 10, 1922–JUNE 22, 1969." Her favorite song was "Through the Years," and the lyric, "I'll come to you smiling through the years." I knew that was perfect with her name. I was able to make certain everything was the way Mama would have wanted.

In January 2017, my mother's earthly remains were removed from Ferncliff and flown to Los Angeles. On Saturday, June 10, 2017, what would have been her ninety-fifth birthday, a small ceremony was held at Hollywood Forever Cemetery, where her body was interred within the Abbey of the Psalms Mausoleum, in a newly named private section called the Judy Garland Pavilion.

Hollywood Forever kindly closed the whole cemetery so that our family could have a private remembrance. I arranged for a small service to commemorate the reinterment with my husband Colin, my best friend Kate Johnson, Michael Feinstein, my two children, and my grandson Logan. Gabriel Ferrer, son of José Ferrer and Rosemary Clooney and an Episcopal priest, officiated. The whole service was half an hour from beginning to end, but it was an important time, especially for my children. They had never known their grandmother, and this was a moment of connection. And, of course, there is space in the Pavilion for all the family: Liza, Joe, myself, and my children and grandchildren. As for Liza and Joe, they wanted to visit by themselves and have their moment alone with Mama. Later that evening, Hollywood Forever opened and held an outdoor screening of *The Wizard of Oz*, which drew 4,000 fans. I loved my mother more than anyone in the world and respected her artistry and genius. I'm incredibly grateful to be her daughter. The overwhelming knowledge that my parents loved me and loved us more than life itself fills my heart with happiness in every moment of my being.

Sharing the family memories and photographs from *A Star Is Born* as well as moving my mother to Hollywood Forever are major events of closure for me. This closure has been empowering. Ironically, I find that the more I let her go, the more I realize she is always with me. A book and a cemetery plot are nice, but as Peter Allen told me nearly fifty years ago, she's not really there. She's no place and she's everywhere. The closest you'll ever get to meeting the adult Judy Garland is by watching *A Star Is Born*. It is, in every sense of the word, a comeback. No matter how many times she's down, she will always come up. The optimism and hope— what we associate with the best of ourselves—will always be there.

Notes

INTRODUCTION

1. Judy Garland, as told to Joe Hyams. "The Real Me," *McCall's* 84, no. 7 (April 1957): 174.

2. *A Star Is Born* (1954) pressbook.

3. "A Star Is Born," *Variety* (September 29, 1954): 6.

4. "New Day for Judy," *Life* 37, no. 11 (September 13, 1954): 163, 165.

5. "The New Pictures: *A Star Is Born*," *Time*, October 25, 1954: 86–87.

6. Bosley Crowther, "Sizing the Entries: Some Current Candidates for the 'Best Films,'" *New York Times* (December 5, 1954): X5.

CHAPTER ONE:

THE BEGINNINGS: *WHAT PRICE HOLLYWOOD?* (1932) *AND A STAR IS BORN* (1937)

1. Gary Carey, *Cukor & Co.: The Films of George Cukor and His Collaborators* (New York: Museum of Modern Art, 1971), 28.

2. Louella O. Parsons, "*Star Is Born* Shows Hollywood as It Is," *Los Angeles Examiner* (April 21, 1937).

3. Ring Lardner Jr. to Ronald Haver in a letter dated June 1992, Ring Lardner Jr. papers, file 42, Margaret Herrick Library, Academy of Motion Picture Arts and Sciences.

4. William Wellman Jr., *Wild Bill Wellman: Hollywood Rebel* (New York: Pantheon, 2015), 328–329.

5. David Thomson, *Showman: The Life of David O. Selznick* (New York: Alfred A. Knopf, 1992), 217.

6. Gavin Lambert, *On Cukor*. Edited by Robert Trachtenberg (New York: Rizzoli, 2000), 41.

7. See David O. Selznick in a memorandum to Daniel T. O'Shea, assistant to Selznick and Secretary of Selznick International, dated January 7, 1937 in Rudy Behlmer, ed. *Memo from David O. Selznick*. (New York: Viking Press, 1972), 108–109 and Wellman Jr., 332.

8. Daniel Selznick, interview with Jeffrey Vance, 2010.

9. William Wellman Jr., interview with Jeffrey Vance, 2010.

CHAPTER TWO:

A STAR IS BORN (1954): THE FILM THAT GOT AWAY

1. Mickey Rooney, interview with Jeffrey Vance, 2010.

2. Judy Garland famously shared this anecdote on *The Jack Parr Program*, which aired on NBC on December 7, 1962. See Randy L. Schmidt, ed., *Judy Garland on Judy Garland: Interviews and Encounters* (Chicago: Chicago Review Press, 2014), 307.

3. Adela Rogers St. Johns, *Some Are Born Great* (New York: Doubleday, 1974), 47.

4. "Judy Garland Slashes Throat After Film Row," *Los Angeles Times* (June 21, 1950): 1.

5. Ronald Haver, *A Star Is Born: The Making of the 1954 Movie and Its 1983 Restoration* (New York: Alfred A. Knopf, 1988), 37.

6. Steven Bach, *Dazzler: The Life and Times of Moss Hart* (New York: Alfred A. Knopf, 2001), 313.

7. Judy Garland, "Judy Garland's Own Story: There'll Always Be an Encore, Part I," *McCall's* 91, no. 4 (January 1964): 142.

8. Gene Allen interview with Jeffrey Vance, 2010.

9. George Cukor in a letter to Katharine Hepburn, George Cukor papers, file 232, Margaret Herrick Library, Academy of Motion Picture Arts and Sciences. This letter is quoted in Haver's history of the film as well as Gerald Clarke's biography of Garland.

10. Jeff Wise and Robert Smith, "An Interview with George Cukor" in Robert Emmet Long, ed., *George Cukor Interviews* (Jackson: University Press of Mississippi, 2001), 90–91.

11. Schmidt, 210.

12. James Mason, *Before I Forget* (London: Hamish Hamilton, 1981), 251.

13. Ibid., 252.

14. Gavin Lambert, *On Cukor*. Edited by Robert Trachtenberg (New York: Rizzoli, 2000), 53–54.

15. Haver, 158.

16. Lambert, 53.

17. George Hoyningen-Huene, "Color Is Used to Suggest Mood in *A Star Is Born*," *New York Herald Tribune* (December 19, 1954).

18. Mason, 248.

19. Gerold Frank, *Judy* (New York: Harper & Row, 1975), 377.

20. Hedda Hopper, "Curtain Going Up to Profile Selwyns," *Los Angeles Times* (July 12, 1954): B6.

21. John Gillett and David Robinson, *Sight and Sound* interview with Cukor from 1964, in Robert Emmet Long, ed., *George Cukor Interviews* (Jackson: University Press of Mississippi, 2001), 10.

22. George Cukor in a letter to Moss Hart dated August 18, 1954, George Cukor papers, file 232, Margaret Herrick Library, Academy of Motion Picture Arts and Sciences.

23. "New Day for Judy," *Life* 37, no. 11 (September 13, 1954): 163–166, 168, 170.

24. The complete film documenting the Hollywood premiere is part of the Warner Home Video DVD/Blu-ray release of *A Star Is Born* published in 2010.

25. Frank, 389.

26. "The New Pictures: *A Star Is Born*," *Time* 64 (October 25, 1954): 86–87.

27. Edwin Schallert, "*Star Is Born* Hit at Lavish Premiere," *Los Angeles Times* (September 30, 1954): A1.

28. Bosley Crowther, "The Rebirth of *A Star*," *New York Times* (October 17, 1954): X1

29. Abel Green, "*A Star Is Born*," *Variety* (September 29, 1954): 6.

30. Noël Coward, *The Noël Coward Diaries*. Edited by Graham Payne and Sheridan Morley (Boston: Little, Brown and Company, 1982), 248–249.

31. Liza Minnelli, interview with Jeffrey Vance, 2011. Minnelli shared the same memory with Ronald Haver. See Haver, 214.

32. Judy Garland as told to Joe Hyams. "The Real Me," *McCall's* 84, no. 7 (April 1957): 175.

33. Lauren Bacall, *By Myself and Then Some* (New York: HarperEntertainment, 2005), 247–248.

34. Aline Mosby, "Judy Feels 'Grateful' Over Oscar Condolences," *New York World Telegram* (April 12, 1955).

35. Anthony Holden, *Behind the Oscar: The Secret History of the Academy Awards* (New York: Plume, 1993), 206.

36. Christopher Finch, *Rainbow: The Stormy Life of Judy Garland* (New York: Grosset & Dunlap, 1975), 201.

37. Lambert, 39.

38. Sid Luft, *Judy and I: My Life with Judy Garland* (Chicago: Chicago Review Press, 2017), 410.

39. Frank, 488.

40. Finch, 217.

41. Dirk Bogarde, *Snakes and Ladders* (London: Holt, Reinhart and Winston, 1979), 260–261.

42. A printed copy of Mason's eulogy is in the collection of Lorna Luft.

CHAPTER THREE:
BARBRA STREISAND'S *A STAR IS BORN* (1976)

1. Marie Brenner, *Going Hollywood: An Insider's Look at the Power and Pretense in the Movie Business* (New York: Delacorte Press, 1978), 73. See also John Gregory Dunne, *Regards: The Selected Nonfiction of John Gregory Dunne* (New York: Thunder's Mouth Press, 2006), 38.

2. "Third Time Around for *Star*—WB to Remake," *Variety* (August 24, 1973): 1.

3. Barbra Streisand commentary track to the Blu-ray release of *A Star Is Born* (1976), Warner Bros. Entertainment, 2004.

4. Christopher Nickens and Karen Swenson. *The Films of Barbra Streisand* (New York: Citadel Press, 2000), 134.

5. Frank Pierson, "My Battles with Barbra and Jon," *New York* (November 15, 1976): 49.

6. James Spada, "On Location: Streisand and Kristofferson Stage a Freak-Out in Phoenix for the New *Star Is Born*," *In The Know* (July 1976): 8.

7. Ibid., 10.

8. Dave Paulson, "Story Behind the Song 'Evergreen,'" *Tennessean* (July 10, 2015).

9. Barbra Streisand's commentary track to the Blu-ray release of *A Star Is Born* (1976), Warner Bros. Entertainment, 2004.

10. Ibid.

11. Ibid.

12. Lawrence B. Eisenberg, "Barbra Streisand: Tough, Temperamental, Tremendous," *Cosmopolitan* (March 1977): 189.

13. James Spada, *Streisand: Her Life* (New York: Crown, 1995), 357.

14. *A Star Is Born* Warner Bros. press release dated March 12, 1976.

15. Frank Pierson, "My Battles with Barbra and Jon," *New York* (November 15, 1976): 60.

16. Charles Champlin, "Barbra Stars in *Star*," *Los Angeles Times* (December 21, 1976): G1.

17. Vincent Canby, "A Film Is Reborn," *New York Times* (December 27, 1976): C16.

18. Pauline Kael, "Contempt for the Audience," *The New Yorker* (January 10, 1977): 94.

19. Neal Gabler, *Barbra Streisand: Redefining Beauty, Femininity, and Power* (New Haven, Conn.: Yale University Press, 2016), 178.

CHAPTER FOUR:

A STAR IS REBORN

1. Janet Staiger, "The Logic of Alternative Readings: *A Star Is Born*" in Staiger, *Interpreting Films* (Princeton, N.J.: Princeton University Press, 1992), 154–177.

2. Judy Garland, "Judy Garland's Own Story: There'll Always Be an Encore, Part II," *McCall's* 91, no. 5 (February 1964): 178.

3. Henry Pleasants, *The Great American Popular Singers* (New York: Simon & Schuster, 1974), 286.

4. George Cukor to Gene Allen in a letter dated January 25, 1979, Gene Allen papers, file 172, Margaret Herrick Library, Academy of Motion Picture Arts and Sciences.

5. Sid Luft, *Judy and I: My Life with Judy Garland* (Chicago: Chicago Review Press, 2017), 449.

6. Finch, 201.

7. Ronald Haver, *A Star Is Born: The Making of the 1954 Movie and Its 1983 Restoration* (New York: Alfred A. Knopf, 1988), 255.

8. David Denby, "*A Star* Comes Back," *New York* (July 25, 1983): 67.

9. Haver, 274.

10. Ibid.

11. Gerald Clarke, *Get Happy: The Life of Judy Garland* (New York: Random House, 2000), 327.

12. Janet Maslin, "Restoration: Save It for the Loveable Movies," *New York Times* (August 28, 1983): H15.

13. Luft, 300.

14. Mickey Rooney, interview with Jeffrey Vance, 2010.

15. Margaret O'Brien, interview with Jeffrey Vance, 2010.

16. Angela Lansbury, interview with Jeffrey Vance, 2010.

17. Lauren Bacall, interview with Jeffrey Vance, 2010.

18. John Fricke, *Judy Garland: A Legendary Film Career* (Philadelphia: Running Press, 2010), 313.

Bibliography

BOOKS AND BROCHURES

Bacall, Lauren. *By Myself and Then Some*. New York: HarperEntertainment, 2005.

Bach, Steven. *Dazzler: The Life and Times of Moss Hart*. New York: Alfred A. Knopf, 2001.

Behlmer, Rudy, ed. *Memo from David O. Selznick*. Introduction by S. N. Behrman. New York: Viking Press, 1972.

Bickford, Charles. *Bulls Balls Bicycles & Actors*. New York: Paul S. Eriksson, 1965.

Bogarde, Dirk. *Snakes and Ladders*. London: Triad Grafton, 1979.

Bordwell, David, Janet Staiger, and Kristin Thompson. *The Classical Hollywood Cinema: Film Style and Mode of Production to 1960*. New York: Columbia University Press, 1985.

Brenner, Marie. *Going Hollywood: An Insider's Look at the Power and Pretense in the Movie Business*. New York: Delacorte Press, 1978.

Carey, Gary. *Cukor & Co.: The Films of George Cukor and His Collaborators*. New York: Museum of Modern Art, 1971.

Carlyle, John. *Under the Rainbow*. Foreword by Robert Osborne. New York: Carroll & Graf Publishers, 2006.

Chaplin, Saul. *The Golden Age of Movie Musicals and Me*. Norman: University of Oklahoma Press, 1994.

Clarke, Gerald. *Get Happy: The Life of Judy Garland*. New York: Random House, 2000.

Coleman, Emily R. *The Complete Judy Garland: The Ultimate Guide to Her Career in Films, Records, Concerts, Radio, and Television, 1935–1969*. New York: Harper & Row, 1990.

Coward, Noël. *The Noël Coward Diaries*. Edited by Graham Payne and Sheridan Morley Boston: Little, Brown and Company, 1982.

Crowther, Bosley. *Hollywood Rajah: The Life and Times of Louis B. Mayer*. New York: Henry Holt and Company, 1960.

Deans, Mickey, and Ann Pinchot. *Weep No More, My Lady*. New York: Hawthorne Books, 1972.

Dunne, John Gregory. *Regards: The Selected Nonfiction of John Gregory Dunne*. Foreword by Calvin Trillin. New York: Thunder's Mouth Press, 2006.

Dyer, Richard. *Heavenly Bodies: Film Stars and Society*. New York: St. Martin's Press, 1986.

Edwards, Anne. *Judy Garland: A Biography*. New York: Simon & Schuster, 1975.

——. *Streisand: A Biography*. Boston: Little, Brown and Company, 1997.

Eyman, Scott. *Lion in Hollywood: The Life and Legend of Louis B. Mayer*. New York: Simon & Schuster, 2005.

Finch, Christopher. *Rainbow: The Stormy Life of Judy Garland*. New York: Grosset & Dunlap, 1975.

Fitzgerald, F. Scott. *The Love of the Last Tycoon*. Preface and notes by Matthew J. Bruccoli. New York: Scribner, 1993.

Frank, Gerold. *Judy*. New York: Harper & Row, 1975.

Fricke, John. *Judy Garland: A Legendary Film Career*. Philadelphia: Running Press, 2010.

——. *Judy Garland: A Portrait in Art & Anecdote*. Foreword by Lorna Luft. New York: Bulfinch Press, 2003.

——. *Judy Garland: World's Greatest Entertainer*. New York: MJF Books, 1992.

Gabler, Neal. *Barbra Streisand: Redefining Beauty, Femininity, and Power*. New Haven, Conn.: Yale University Press, 2016.

——. *An Empire of Their Own: How the Jews Invented Hollywood*. New York: Crown, 1988.

Gershwin, Ira. *Lyrics on Several Occasions*. New York: Viking Press, 1973.

Gledhill, Christine, ed. *Stardom: Industry of Desire*. New York: Routledge, 1991.

Granger, Stewart. *Sparks Fly Upward*. New York: G.P. Putnam's Sons, 1981.

Hart, Moss. *Act One: An Autobiography*. New York: Random House, 1959.

Hart, Moss, and George S. Kaufman. *Once in a Lifetime*. New York: Farrar & Rinehart, 1930.

Haver, Ronald. *David O. Selznick's Hollywood*. New York: Alfred A. Knopf, 1980.

——. *A Star Is Born: The Making of the 1954 Movie and Its 1983 Restoration*. New York: Alfred A. Knopf, 1988.

Hepburn, Katharine. *Me: Stories of My Life*. New York: Alfred A. Knopf, 1991.

Hofler, Robert. *Sexplosion: From Andy Warhol to A Clockwork Orange—How a Generation of Pop Rebels Broke All the Taboos*. New York: HarperCollins, 2014.

Holden, Anthony. *Behind the Oscar: The Secret History of the Academy Awards*. New York: Simon & Schuster, 1993.

Icons and Idols, Julien's Auctions Catalogue. Culver City, Calif.: Julien Entertainment, November 17, 2017.

Jablonski, Edward. *Harold Arlen: Happy with the Blues*. Garden City, N.Y.: Doubleday & Company, 1961.

Kaufman, George S., and Marc Connelly. *Merton of the Movies. A Dramatization of Harry Leon Wilson's Story of the Same Name*. New York: Samuel French, 1925.

Kimball, Robert, ed. *The Complete Lyrics of Ira Gershwin*. New York: Alfred A. Knopf, 1993.

Lambert, Gavin. *On Cukor*. Edited by Robert Trachtenberg. New York: Rizzoli International, 2000.

Lazar, Irving, with Annette Tapert. *Swifty: My Life and Good Times*. New York: Simon & Schuster, 1995.

Lev, Peter. *History of the American Cinema, Vol. 7: Transforming the Screen, 1950–1959*. Charles Harpole, general editor. New York: Charles Scribner's Sons, 2003.

Levy, Emanuel. *George Cukor, Master of Elegance: Hollywood's Legendary Director and His Stars*. New York: William Morrow and Company, 1994.

Long, Robert Emmet. *George Cukor Interviews*. Jackson: University Press of Mississippi, 2001.

Luft, Lorna. *Me and My Shadows: A Family Memoir*. New York: Pocket Books, 1998.

Luft, Sid. *Judy and I: My Life with Judy Garland*. Foreword by Randy L. Schmidt. Chicago: Chicago Review Press, 2017.

Martin, Hugh. *Hugh Martin: The Boy Next Door*. Foreword by Michael Feinstein. Encinitas, Cal.: Trolley Press, 2010.

Mason, James. *Before I Forget*. London: Hamish Hamilton, 1981.

McGilligan, Patrick. *George Cukor: A Double Life*. New York: St. Martin's Press, 1991.

Meyer, John. *Heartbreaker*. Garden City, N.Y.: Doubleday & Company, 1983.

Minnelli, Vincente, with Hector Acre. *I Remember It Well*. Foreword by Alan Jay Lerner. Garden City, N.Y.: Doubleday, 1974.

Morella, Joe, and Edward Z. Epstein. *The Films and Career of Judy Garland*. New York: Citadel Press, 1969.

Nickens, Christopher, and Karen Swenson. *The Films of Barbra Streisand*. New York: Citadel Press, 2000.

Osborne, Robert. *85 Years of the Oscar: The Official History of the Academy Awards*. New York: Abbeville Press, 2013.

Pasternak, Joe, as told to David Chandler. *Easy the Hard Way*. New York: G.P. Putnam's Sons, 1956.

Peary, Danny. *Alternate Oscars: One Critic's Defiant Choices for Best Picture, Actor, and Actress from 1927 to the Present*. New York: Dell Publishing, 1993.

——. *Cult Movies 3: 50 More of the Classics, the Sleepers, the Weird and the Wonderful*. New York: Simon & Schuster, 1988.

Pleasants, Henry. *The Great American Popular Singers*. New York: Simon & Schuster, 1974.

Powdermaker, Hortense. *Hollywood the Dream Factory: An Anthropologist Looks at the Movie-Makers*. Boston: Little, Brown and Company, 1950.

Rooney, Mickey. *Life is Too Short*. New York: Villard Books, 1991.

Russo, Vito. *The Celluloid Closet: Homosexuality in the Movies*, rev. ed. New York: Harper & Row, 1987.

Sanders, Coyne Steven. *Rainbow's End: The Judy Garland Show*. New York: William Morrow and Company, 1990.

Schechter, Scott. *Judy Garland: The Day-By-Day Chronicle of a Legend*. New York: Cooper Square Press, 2002.

Schickel, Richard. *The Men Who Made the Movies: Interviews with Frank Capra, George Cukor, Howard Hawks, Alfred Hitchcock, Vincente Minnelli, King Vidor, Raoul Walsh, and William A. Wellman*. New York: Atheneum, 1975.

Schmidt, Randy L., ed. *Judy Garland on Judy Garland: Interviews and Encounters*. Chicago: Chicago Review Press, 2014.

Schulberg, Budd. *What Makes Sammy Run?* New York: Random House, 1941.

Selznick, Irene Mayer. *A Private View*. New York: Alfred A. Knopf, 1983.

Sharaff, Irene. *Broadway & Hollywood: Costumes Designed by Irene Sharaff*. New York: Van Nostrand Reinhold Company, 1976.

Smyth, J. E. *Reconstructing American Historical Cinema: From Cimarron to Citizen Kane*. Lexington: University Press of Kentucky, 2006.

Spada, James. *Streisand: Her Life*. New York: Crown Publishers, 1995.

Sperling, Cass Warner, and Cork Milner with Jack Warner Jr. *Hollywood Be Thy Name: The Warner Brothers Story*. Rocklin, Calif.: Prima Publishing, 1994.

St. Johns, Adela Rogers. *Some Are Born Great*. New York: Doubleday & Company, 1974.

Staiger, Janet. *Interpreting Films*. Princeton, N.J.: Princeton University Press, 1992.

A Star Is Born program book. Los Angeles: Alan Lithographers/Academy of Motion Pictures Arts and Sciences, 1983.

Stratton, James. *A Star Is Born & Born Again: Variation on a Hollywood Archetype*. Albany, Ga.: BearManor Media, 2015.

Thomas, Bob. *Clown Price of Hollywood: The Antic Life and Times of Jack L. Warner*. New York: McGraw-Hill Publishing, 1990.

Thompson, Frank T. *William A. Wellman*. Foreword by Barbara Stanwyck. Metuchen, N.J.: Scarecrow Press, 1983.

Thomson, David. *Showman: The Life of David O. Selznick*. New York: Alfred A. Knopf, 1992.

———. *Warner Bros: The Making of an American Movie Studio*. New Haven: Yale University Press, 2017.

Tormé, Mel. *The Other Side of the Rainbow with Judy Garland on the Dawn Patrol*. New York: Galahad Books, 1970.

Warner, Jack L., with Dean Jennings. *My First Hundred Years in Hollywood*. New York: Random House, 1965.

Watson, Thomas J., and Bill Chapman. *Judy: Portrait of an American Legend*. New York: McGraw-Hill Book Company, 1986.

Watts, Stephen, ed. *Behind the Screen: How Films Are Made*. New York: Dodge Publishing Company, 1938.

Wellman, William A. *A Short Time for Insanity*. Foreword by Richard Schickel. New York: Hawthorn Books, 1974.

Wellman, William Jr. *Wild Bill Wellman: Hollywood Rebel*. New York: Pantheon Books, 2015.

West, Nathanael. *The Day of the Locust*. New York: Random House, 1939.

Willoughby, Bob. *The Star Makers: On Set with Hollywood's Greatest Directors*. Foreword by Sydney Pollack. New York: Merrell, 2003.

NEWSPAPER AND PERIODICAL ARTICLES

Aaronson, Charles S. "*A Star Is Born.*" *Motion Picture Herald*, October 2, 1954, 22.

Archerd, Army. "Barbra Farewells Ray Stark; Future as She Dictates." *Variety*, July 17, 1974, 6.

"The Big Build-Up." *Harper's Bazaar* (November 1954): 121.

Canby, Vincent. "A Film Is Reborn." *New York Times*, December 27, 1976, C16.

Carroll, Harrison. "Judy Garland in Supreme Triumph!" *Los Angeles Herald-Express*, September 30, 1954, A22.

Cerf, Bennett. "Trade Winds: Babes in Hollywood." *Saturday Review* 37 (October 23, 1954): 8.

Champlin, Charles. "Barbra Stars in *Star*." *Los Angeles Times*, December 21, 1976, G1.

Clurman, Harold. "Punch and Judy." *New Republic* 125 (November 26, 1951): 21–22.

Cocks, Jay. "Barbra, a One-Woman Hippodrome." *Time* 109 (January 3, 1977), 62.

Crowther, Bosley. "*A Star Is Born* Bows." *New York Times*, October 12, 1954, 23.

———. "The Rebirth of *a Star*." *New York Times*, October 17, 1954, X1.

——. "Sizing the Entries: Some Current Candidates for the 'Best Films.'" *New York Times*, December 5, 1954, X5.

Denby, David. "*A Star* Comes Back." *New York* (July 25, 1983): 67–68.

Eisenberg, Lawrence B. "Barbra Streisand: Tough, Temperamental, Tremendous." *Cosmopolitan* (March 1977): 189.

"Film Reviews: *A Star Is Born*." *Films in Review* 5 (November 1954): 479–481.

"Filmland's Top Stars Attend *A Star Is Born* Premiere." *Los Angeles Examiner*, September 30, 1954, III, 1.

Garland, Judy. "Judy Garland's Own Story: There'll Always Be an Encore, Part I." *McCall's* 91, no. 4 (January 1964): 54–57, 141–144.

——. "Judy Garland's Own Story: There'll Always Be an Encore, Part II." *McCall's* 91, no. 5 (February 1964): 64, 177–178.

Garland, Judy, as told to Joe Hyams. "The Real Me." *McCall's* 84, no. 7 (April 1957): 78–80, 171–173, 175.

Goldman, William. "Judy Floats." *Esquire* 71, no. 1 (January 1969): 78–80.

Green, Abel. "*A Star is Born*" *Variety*, September 29, 1954, 6.

Gross, Michael Joseph. "The Queen Is Dead." *Atlantic Monthly* (August 2000): 62–70.

Harmetz, Aljean. "Missing 'Star' Is Found. *New York Times*, April 15, 1983, C10.

——. "*Rear Window* Success Inspires Other Reissues." *New York Times*, October 31, 1983, C15.

Harvey, Stephen. "Thanks to a Sleuth, *A Star Is Born* Takes a New Lease on Life." *New York Times*, July 3, 1983, H11, H12.

Haver, Ronald. "*A Star Is Born* Again." *American Film* 8, no. 9 (July–August 1983): 28–33, 59.

Hopper, Hedda. "Curtain Going Up to Profile Selwyns." *Los Angeles Times*, July 12, 1954, B6.

——. "Judy Garland Obtains Release from Studio." *Los Angeles Times*, September 30, 1950, 3.

Hoyningen-Huene, George. "Color Is Used to Suggest Mood in *A Star Is Born*." *New York Herald Tribune*, December 19, 1954.

Hyams, Joe. "Crack-Up." *Photoplay* 51, no. 1 (January 1957): 38–41, 60–62.

Jewel, Richard. "RKO Film Grosses: 1931–1951." *Historical Journal of Film Radio and Television* 14, no. 1 (1994), 39.

"Judy Garland, 47, Found Dead." *New York Times*, June 23, 1969, 1, 31.

"Judy Garland Slashes Throat After Film Row." *Los Angeles Times*, June 21, 1950, 1, 4.

Kael, Pauline. "Contempt for the Audience." *New Yorker* (January 10, 1977): 89–90, 93–94.

Kane, Sherwin. "*A Star Is Born*." *Motion Picture Daily* 76, no. 63 (September 29, 1954): 1, 3.

La Badie, Donald. "*A Star Is Born*: A *Film Daily* Review." *The Film Daily* (September 29, 1954): 7.

Maslin, Janet. "Restoration: Save It for the Loveable Movies." *New York Times*, August 28, 1983, H15, H18.

McMurty, Larry. "The Disappearance of Love." *American Film* 2, no. 8 (June 1977): 6–7, 61.

Michaelson, Judith. "Industry Pays Homage to a Restored *Star*." *Los Angeles Times*, July 21, 1983, IV1,6.

Mosby, Aline. "Judy Feels 'Grateful' Over Oscar Condolences." *New York World Telegram*, April 12, 1955.

Murphy, A.D. "*A Star Is Born*." *Variety*, December 22, 1976, 20.

"New Day for Judy." *Life* 37, no. 11 (September 13, 1954): 163–166, 168, 170.

"New Films: Triumph for Hollywood." *Newsweek* 44 (November 1, 1954): 86–87.

"The New Pictures: *A Star Is Born*." *Time* 64 (October 25, 1954): 86–87.

Nugent, Frank S. "*A Star Is Born*." *New York Times*, April 23, 1937, 25.

Parsons, Louella O. "*Star Is Born* Shows Hollywood as It Is." *Los Angeles Examiner*, April 21, 1937.

Paulson, Dave. "Story Behind the Song 'Evergreen.'" *Tennessean*, July 10, 2015.

Pierson, Frank. "My Battles with Barbra and Jon." *New West* (November 22, 1976): 27–44.

———. "My Battles with Barbra and Jon." *New York* (November 15, 1976): 49–60.

"Rites Conducted for Judy Garland's Mother." *Los Angeles Times*, January 9, 1953, A1.

Schallert, Edwin. "*Star Is Born* Hit at Lavish Premiere." *Los Angeles Times*, September 30, 1954, A1.

Scheuer, Philip K. "Star Judy Garland Is 'Born' Again in Film's New Version." *Los Angeles Times*, August 29, 1954, D1.

"Show Business: Séance at the Palace." *Time* 90 (August 18, 1967): 40.

Silverman, Sime. "*What Price Hollywood*." *Variety*, July 17, 1932.

Spada, James. "On Location: Streisand and Kristofferson Stage A Freak-Out in Phoenix for the New *Star Is Born*." *In The Know* (July 1976): 8–10.

Spear, Ivan. "Warner's *A Star Is Born* Is a Showman's Picture." *Box Office* (October 2, 1954): 26.

"*A Star Is Born*." *Variety*, April 28, 1937, 15.

Stewart, Garrett. "The Woman in the Moon." *Sight & Sound* 46, no. 3 (Summer 1977): 177–181, 185.

"Third Time Around for *Star*—WB to Remake." *Variety*, August 24, 1973, 1.

Thomas, Kevin. "3 Decades Later, *Star* Is Reborn." *Los Angeles Times*, July 17, 1983, Calendar 18–19.

"*What Price Hollywood?*" *New York Times*, July 16, 1932, 5.

"*What Price Hollywood?*" *Variety*, July 19, 1932, 24.

AUTHOR'S INTERVIEWS

Gene Allen, interview with Jeffrey Vance, 2010.

Lauren Bacall, interview with Jeffrey Vance, 2010.

Tony Bennett, interview with Jeffrey Vance, 2010.

Leslie Caron, interview with Jeffrey Vance, 2011.

Carleton Carpenter, interview with Jeffrey Vance, 2011.

Olivia de Havilland, interview with Jeffrey Vance, 2011.

Norman Jewison, interview with Jeffrey Vance, 2011.

Sally Kirkland, interview with Jeffrey Vance, 2011.

Miles Kreuger, interview with Jeffrey Vance, 2011.

Angela Lansbury, interview with Jeffrey Vance, 2010.

Jerry Lewis, interview with Jeffrey Vance, 2010.

Mort Lindsey, interview with Jeffrey Vance, 2010.

Jerry Maren, interview with Jeffrey Vance, 2010.

Hugh Martin, interview with Jeffrey Vance, 2010.

Liza Minnelli, interview with Jeffrey Vance, 2011.

Kim Novak, interview with Jeffrey Vance, 2011.

Margaret O'Brien, interview with Jeffrey Vance, 2010.

Robert Osborne, interview with Jeffrey Vance, 2010.

Frank Pierson, interview with Jeffrey Vance, 2010.

Jane Powell, interview with Jeffrey Vance, 2010.

Debbie Reynolds, interview with Jeffrey Vance, 2011.

Mickey Rooney, interview with Jeffrey Vance, 2010.

Ann Rutherford, interview with Jeffrey Vance, 2010.

Eva Marie Saint, interview with Jeffrey Vance, 2010.

Coyne Steven Sanders, interview with Jeffrey Vance, 2010.

George Schlatter, interview with Jeffrey Vance, 2011.

Daniel Selznick, interview with Jeffrey Vance, 2010.

David Shepard, interview with Jeffrey Vance, 2010.

Bob Thomas, interview with Jeffrey Vance, 2010.

William Wellman Jr., interview with Jeffrey Vance, 2010.

ARCHIVAL COLLECTIONS, DOCUMENTS, AND MISCELLANEOUS

Gene Allen papers, Margaret Herrick Library, Academy of Motion Picture Arts and Sciences.

George Cukor Collection, University of Southern California Cinematic Arts Library.

George Cukor papers, Margaret Herrick Library, Academy of Motion Picture Arts and Sciences.

Harry B. Friedman papers, Margaret Herrick Library, Academy of Motion Picture Arts and Sciences.

Judy Garland private audio recordings 1963–1966, Lorna Luft Collection.

Ronald Haver Collection, Margaret Herrick Library, Academy of Motion Picture Arts and Sciences.

Fay and Michael Kanin papers, Margaret Herrick Library, Academy of Motion Picture Arts and Sciences.

Ring Lardner Jr. papers, Margaret Herrick Library, Academy of Motion Picture Arts and Sciences.

David O. Selznick Collection, Harry Ransom Center, University of Texas at Austin.

A Star Is Born (1937) pressbook.

A Star Is Born (1954) pressbook.

A Star Is Born (1976) pressbook.

A Star Is Born daily production and progress reports, August 13, 1953–July 29, 1954, USC Warner Bros. Archives, University of Southern California Cinematic Arts Library.

USC Warner Bros. Archives, University of Southern California Cinematic Arts Library.

Jack L. Warner Collection, University of Southern California Cinematic Arts Library.

Photo Credits

All photographs courtesy Lorna Luft and Independent Visions, except as follows:

Matt Tunia Collection: Pages 186, 189–192, 195, 198

WENN Ltd./Alamy Stock Photo: Page 225

John Engstead/mptv: Pages 5, 6, 11

Sandford Roth/mptv: Pages 2, 3, 80, 81, 91, 100, 101, 213

Bob Willoughby/mptv: Pages 8, 15, 52, 55, 88, 93, 94, 105, 123, 133, 216

John Engstead, Sandford Roth, Bob Willoughby, and Independent Visions are exclusively represented by mptv. For more information regarding licensing or purchasing images from mptv, please contact mptvimages as www.mptvimages.com.

While every effort has been made to identify the proper photographer and/or copyright owners, some images had no accreditation. In these instances, if proper credit and copyright is determined, credits will be added in subsequent printings.

What Price Hollywood? © **Warner Bros. Entertainment**

A Star Is Born (1954) © **Warner Bros. Entertainment**

A Star Is Born (1976) © **Warner Bros. Entertainment**

Acknowledgments

I WOULD LIKE TO EXPRESS MY HEARTFELT THANKS TO THOSE WHO HAVE SUPPORTED me in writing this book. First and foremost, my children: my son, Jesse Cole Richards, and his wife, Jaimee Richards, and my daughter, Vanessa Jade Richards, and her partner, Patrick O'Neill; my grandchildren, Jordan Eloise Richards, Luke Kanan Richards, and Logan Jake O'Neill. To my husband, Colin R. Freeman; my gorgeous chocolate Labrador, Lowe; my sister, Liza Minnelli; my brother Joe Luft; my manager Garry Kief and everyone at Stiletto Entertainment; my agent Alan Nevins and everyone at Renaissance Literary & Talent; my publicist Victoria Varela. To my treasured friends: Barry Manilow, Michael Feinstein, Terrence Flannery, Kate Edelman Johnson, Joe Benincasa and the Actors Fund of America, John Fricke, Kevin and Brent Bass, Scott Nevins, Marc Hulett, Dr. David Agus, Dr. Philomena McAndrew, Dr. Ray Chu, Dr. Behrooz Hakimian, Dr. Gerald Steiner, Liz and Alan Wyatt, Charles Hart, Nigel and Stacey Green, Shirley and Ramon Greene, Alan and Arlene Lazare, Rob Bagshaw, and the late Robert Osborne.

Finally, I'd like to acknowledge the encouragement I've received from the Actors Fund of America, Ben Mankiewicz, and Turner Classic Movies, and the many fans of *A Star Is Born* who have written to me or approached me on the street to share with me how much they love my mother's film.

—LORNA LUFT, Rancho Mirage, California 2018

I CAME TO TRULY APPRECIATE *A STAR IS BORN* (1954) AFTER BEING REINTRODUCED to it in 2005 by a person whom, at the time, I was quite enamored with. Like many before me, I learned the same hard lesson that Esther Blodgett/Vicki Lester learned. Sometimes love isn't enough. However, *A Star Is Born* remains a sentimental favorite for precisely this reason and I was honored to be asked by Lorna Luft to undertake the project. I thank her for the opportunity.

A special debt of gratitude is due to Jon S. Bouker, my oldest friend and attorney, who went above and beyond serving as an editor and advisor. A special thank-you to Manoah Bowman. His insight and efforts on this book and others remind me how much time has actually passed: twenty years and counting. I am grateful to Sloan De Forest for her help shaping the text, Matt Tunia for assuming the responsibility for all the book's photography, Frank Vlastnik for his assistance with images, and Allen London, who served as the book's researcher. Also, a special thanks for two individuals who are no longer with us: Robert B. Cushman and David Shepard. Their loss was felt throughout the process of writing this book but their memories and love for this film contributed to its creation.

I am grateful to the staff of the Academy of Motion Picture Arts and Sciences' Margaret Herrick Library for their help, in particular Jenny Romero, Stacey Behlmer, and Louise Hilton; Miles Kreuger of the Institute of the American Musical; Sandra M. Garcia-Myers and Edward Comstock of the USC Cinematic Arts Library and George Feltenstein and Ned Price of Warner Bros. At Running Press I'd like to thank our editor Cindy De La Hoz and designer Susan Van Horn. Their contributions were essential to bringing this book to life.

Finally, I would also like to express my particular appreciation for the support I have received in friendship, interest, and encouragement, from Frank Bowling, Bill Daly, Vincent De Paul; Kim A. DeGiralomo; David Eaton, James and Kristine Hall; Frank Labrador; Paul Lekakis; Randal Malone; John Martens, Brandon MacKay; Sean McHugh; Kevin and Michelle Murphy; the late Coyne Steven Sanders; Tracy Terhune; and George Thomas Vance. Finally, a heartfelt thank-you to my sister, Megan Vance, and my mother, Sandra B. Vance.

—JEFFREY VANCE, Los Angeles, California 2018

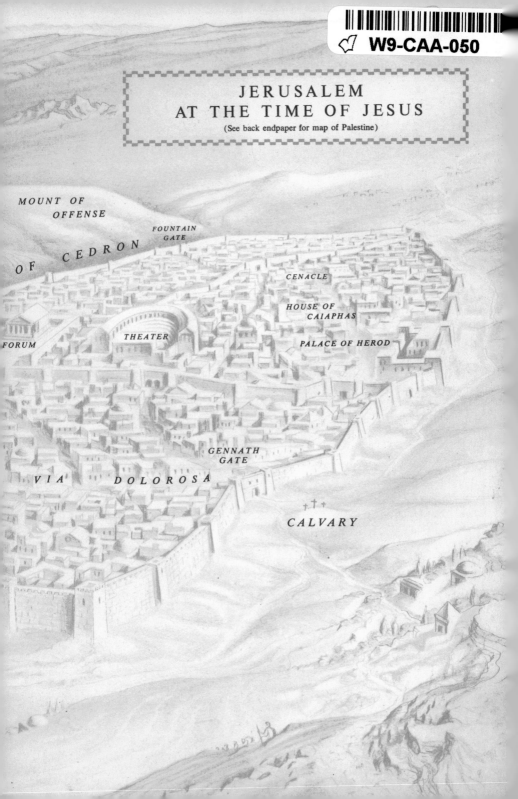

JERUSALEM
AT THE TIME OF JESUS
(See back endpaper for map of Palestine)

MOUNT OF
OFFENSE

FOUNTAIN
GATE

OF CEDRON

CENACLE

HOUSE OF
CAIAPHAS

FORUM

THEATER

PALACE OF HEROD

GENNATH
GATE

VIA DOLOROSA

CALVARY